NATURALISM
AND
ONTOLOGY

### Ridgeview Publishing Company Books
### by Wilfrid Sellars

*Philosophical Perspectives: History of Philosophy (1977)*

*Philosophical Perspectives: Metaphysics and Epistemology (1977)*

*Naturalism and Ontology (1980 and 1997)*

*Pure Pragmatics and Possible Worlds: The Early Essays of Wilfrid Sellars (1980)*

*The Metaphysics of Epistemology: Lectures by Wilfrid Sellars (1989)*

*Science, Perception and Reality (1991)*

*Science and Metaphysics (1992)*

*Kant and Pre-Kantian Themes: Lectures by Wilfrid Sellars (2002)*

*Kant's Transcendental Metaphysics: Sellars' Cassirer Lectures and Other Essays (2002)*

*Wilfrid Sellars Notre Dame Lectures 1969-1986*

# NATURALISM
# AND
# ONTOLOGY

*The John Dewey Lectures for 1974*

## Wilfrid Sellars

Ridgeview Publishing Company    Atascadero, California

Paper text: ISBN 0-917930-16-9

Published in the United States of America
by Ridgeview Publishing Company
Box 686
Atascadero, California 93423
www.ridgeviewpublishing.com

# CONTENTS

## ACKNOWLEDGMENTS

To D. Reidel Publishing Company for permission to print a revision of "Meaning as Functional Classification," in *Intentionality, Language and Translation* edited by J. G. Troyer and S. C. Wheeler, III (Dordrecht, Holland, 1974).

# PREFACE

1. This volume is a revised and expanded version of the John Dewey Lectures given at the University of Chicago in May 1974. As presented, they were an attempt to bring together in a reasonably systematic form certain views on ontology, semantics and the philosophy of mind which I had developed over the previous thirty years. By saying this I do not mean to imply that the many papers in which I presented these views were externally related—that the views in question were not only distinguishable but separable, not only separable but separate—for I have from the beginning been only too aware of their essential interconnectedness. The truth is, rather, that each paper, whichever its central theme, attempted to deal not only with it, but with its place in the scheme of things entire. The inevitable result was that the advantage for the reader of a detailed treatment of a specific topic was diluted by the necessity of grasping its connection with an encompassing, but highly schematic, background theory. Thus, each paper presupposed all the others, as would an atlas published seriatim, or a set of dinnerware picked up piece by piece at the bank. It became clear that sooner or later I would have to bite the bullet and exchange the excitement of free-wheeling voyages of discovery for the mixed pleasures of rational reconstruction.
2. In preparing these lectures for publication, I have attempted to carry even further the task of making explicit the systematic nature of my views. The entering wedge of the argument—Chapters 1 through 3—has been left largely untouched, save for stylistic and editorial changes, but its concluding stages, and in particular the discussions of meaning, mapping and the mental, have been presented in much

greater detail and new material added. I have also included a revised version of the central sections of "Meaning as Functional Classification."[1] The latter is, in my opinion, the best statement in short compass of my views on the nature of meaning. I believe, however, that by being placed in the larger context of this book, and, in particular, by being related to ontological issues pertaining to predication, the points it makes acquire their true significance.

3. In a sense, then, I am saying that this book contains little that is *really* new about my philosophical views. A reader who has struggled through some of my recent papers is bound to have a sense of *deja vu*. The same is true of the reader who has with difficulty penetrated the Kantian wrappings of a preceding attempt at synthesis.[2] Yet in a deeper sense it is all new. For in philosophy it is the argument which counts, and the argument is, indeed, new. It seeks to be self-contained, and to follow its own momentum with a minimum of promissory notes and "as I have argued elsewhere." Unfortunately, of course, the latter cannot be entirely eliminated. For even this attempt at a synthesis has been torn from a larger context, and points to a still larger synthesis which it, too, can only adumbrate. There is always one more *Critique*! But the best is always the enemy of the good, and the complete of the incomplete. Philosophy is surely the paradigm of that which always becomes but never is.

4. I can not close these remarks without thanking those whose published and unpublished comments on my work have given me a genuine sense of participating in a dialogue. The list is long, too long, indeed, to print without an appearance of self-flattery. They know, both individually and collectively, who they are; and to them I say: Thank you.

Pittsburgh, October 25, 1978

---

[1] In *Intentionality, Language and Translation*, J. C. Troyer and S. C. Wheeler, III (eds) (D. Reidel Publishing Company: Dordrecht, Holland, 1974).
[2] *Science and Metaphysics*. The present book may also be of assistance to the student of Kant who finds it difficult to penetrate the Sellarsian wrappings of Kantian themes in *SM*, but who nevertheless senses that the latter might throw some light on the *Critique*.

# INTRODUCTION

1. When I was coming to philosophical consciousness, the great battles between the systems which began the Twentieth Century were drawing to a close, although the lightning and the thunder were still impressive. I cut my teeth on issues dividing Idealist and Realist and, indeed, the various competing forms of upstart Realism. I saw them at the beginning through my father's eyes, and perhaps for that reason never got into Pragmatism. He regarded it as shifty, ambiguous, and indecisive. One thinks in this connection of Lovejoy's "thirteen varieties," though that, my father thought, would make too tidy a picture.

2. "Time is unreal." "Sense data are constituents of physical objects." "Mind is a distinct substance." "We intuit essences." These are issues you can get your teeth into. By contrast, Pragmatism seemed all method and no results.

3. After striking out on my own, I spent my early years fighting in the war against Positivism—the last of the great metaphysical systems; always a realist, flirting with Oxford Aristotelianism, Platonism, Intuitionism, but somehow convinced, at the back of my mind, that something very much like Critical Realism and Evolutionary Naturalism was true.

4. Thus it wasn't until my thought began to crystallize that I really encountered Dewey and began to study him. It certainly wasn't easy going, lacking as he does, the sometimes deceptive clarity of the British Empiricists, though lucidity itself compared to Hegel. He caught me at a time when I was moving away from "the Myth of the Given" (antecedent reality?) and rediscovering the coherence theory of meaning. Thus it was Dewey's Idealistic background which intrigued me the most. I found similar themes in Royce and later in Peirce. I was astonished at what I had missed.

5. Although I count myself a Scientific Realist, Dewey's world of experience is very much akin to what I have called the Manifest Image of man-in-the-world, which, properly understood, is the gateway to Scientific Realism.

6. One of my father's early papers was called "Whose Experience?." He implied that the answer had to be "your experience" or "my experience." But Dewey, of course, would have replied "our experience"—for intersubjectivity and community were at the center of his thought as they are of mine.

7. As for Naturalism. That, too, had negative overtones at home. It was as wishy-washy and ambiguous as Pragmatism. One could believe *almost* anything about the world and even *some* things about God, and yet be a Naturalist. What was needed was a new, nonreductive materialism. My father could call himself a Materialist in all good conscience, for at that time he was about the only one in sight. I, however, do not own the term, and I am so surprised by some of the views of the *new*, new Materialists, that until the dust settles, I prefer the term 'Naturalism', which, while retaining its methodological connotations, has acquired a substantive content, which, if it does not entail scientific realism, is at least not incompatible with it.

# 1  IN PRAISE OF 'something'

1.      Ontology is the theory of what there is. To understand what ontology is, therefore, we must understand the phrase 'what there is', which points to the question 'What is there?' Obviously, if someone were asked this question out of the blue, he would not know what to make of it—unless he were a philosopher, for philosophers carry around with them a context or ambience in which otherwise startling questions are relevant and at home. In this case, however, even if we are in a philosophical mood we can not help but be puzzled by the above question, if we linger for a moment, and don't rush to specific issues in ontology.

2.      At this point I might discuss the grammar of 'what' questions, or call attention to the fact that in ordinary contexts we would feel the question to be incomplete, expecting some such continuation as

[What is there] which has 12 pairs of legs and eats chicken?

Instead I will make the obvious point that when the ontologist asks this question (if he ever does), he is concerned with *kinds*. As is so often the case, a grammatical singular at the surface carries plurality in the depths.

3.      On the other hand, a paraphrase of the initial question as 'What kinds of thing are there?' would (and should) be met with resistance. Thus an ontologist might well object that his concern is not with what *kinds* of things there are, for this admits as answers names of kinds—thus 'lionkind' and 'dragonhood'—and although these might be of interest to him as zoologist or mythologist and, when pondering other questions, even as a logician or philosopher, nevertheless, when,

as an ontologist, he asks 'What is there?', he is not looking for kinds regardless of whether or not they are empty—which is not to say that the kind, empty kind, itself by no means empty, might not be of great interest.

4.      From his point of view, then, a more adequate paraphrase would be

What kinds are there such that there are things of those kinds?

Yet, although this answer has the virtues of leading eventually to such cases as

There are lions
There are tame tigers
There are no dragons,

it obviously begins at a high level of abstraction.

5.      As a matter of fact, it should strike us that our original question might as well have been

What are there?

to which

There are lions, etc.

seems to be a direct answer. And if this answer is brushed aside by someone who asks 'Who cares *qua* ontologist, if there are lions or for that matter dragons?', the following answers might be forthcoming:

There are numbers. There are classes. There are attributes. There are propositions. There are possible worlds.

or

There are classes and classes of classes—but no attributes.

6.      At this point I might turn my attention to the classical distinction between

ordinary kinds and categories. But instead of addressing myself directly to this topic, I prefer to have it take its own time to emerge in the course of these lectures. On the other hand I do want to plunge directly into ontological waters. Or, to change metaphors, into the ontological dialogue which is swirling around us with all its familiar twists and turns. It is my purpose to join the argument—but cagily to choose my moments in such a way as to display my own views to their best advantage.

7.      I shall assume to start with, then, that the way to make a direct ontological commitment to numbers is to say in all candor

There are numbers.

If I were to add 'or something which can reasonably be said to entail this statement' I would, of course, have opened Pandora's Box—and we are not quite ready for *that*. Thus I focus attention to begin with on the form

There are Ks

where 'K' represents a "sortal" or "count noun."

8.      I shall also assume that, to use an example,

There are lions

can be paraphrased as

Something is a lion.

I shall not, however, draw upon the paraphrase

Lions exist

not because it doesn't, at least in some contexts, serve this purpose, but because the verb 'to exist' is a slippery one and has uses which belong in quite different contexts and raise quite different problems.

9.      My general strategy will be to draw a distinction between an interpretation

of such ostensibly philosophical questions as

Are there Ks? e.g., Are there attributes?

according to which the appropriate answer is, so to speak, a truistic 'yes—*of course* there are attributes', and a sense in which the answer, whether yes or no, is highly controversial. This second sense can be phrased in traditional philosophical style as

Are there *really* attributes?

though just what the burden of 'really' is, is part of a longer story. You may be put in mind of Carnap's distinction between "internal" and "external" questions, but this is not what I have in mind, although it is not unrelated, and I shall have something to say about it at a later stage in the argument.

10.    I have implied that in a sense it is a truism to say that there are classes, attributes, numbers, propositions, etc. What is not truistic is, in the spirit of G. E. Moore, the *analysis* of these truisms. Thus, are attributes "analyzable into," or "reducible to," items belonging to another and, presumably, non-abstract kind? Or, to use a more contemporary turn of phrase, are statements about attributes paraphrasable in a philosophically interesting way in terms of statements about non-abstract entities? Can we *regiment* discourse about attributes along nominalistic lines without losing our ability to "say what we want to say." Only as a last resort would I consent to expunge discourse about attributes from my vocabulary. It may indeed turn out to have more straitlaced cousins who can do all the work it *really* does. But appearances are what give point to life—even for the philosopher—and I know that even that admirer of desert landscapes, Quine, enjoys them all the more because of his geographer's knowledge of the jungle.

11.    To return to the main theme. It will be useful to make a terminological commitment and so use the words 'object' and 'classify' that such a statement as

Tom is a man

will be said to refer to an object and to classify it as a man. I remind you that though I am focusing attention on the form x is a K,

I might have used the more general form

x is φ

where 'φ' can represent either a sortal or an adjectival predicate or, even,

φx

where 'φ' can also represent a verb. But the varieties of predication (or what is called predication) and the varieties of use given to the copula are so manifold that it will be good strategy to cut them down to size where this promises even temporary assistance. Notice that by stipulating a use for 'object', I made it possible to reserve 'entity' for a different—if related—role.

12.     How, then, are we to understand

Something is a lion?

Clearly it doesn't refer to a selected object yet it has something to do with objects. If we reflect that the statement in question is true if and only if some object or other is a lion, we may be tempted to say, that in this context, 'something' makes an indefinite or indeterminate reference to objects. To *all* objects (at least of some relevant category)? Well, not in the way

Everything is a lion

does. Yet in its own way it doesn't leave any out. If asked to explain this indeterminate reference to all objects, there are two general lines we might take, the first of which divides into two sub-strategies, each of which points hopefully to the other.

13.     The first general line, (A), argues that the referential character of 'something' is *derivative* from the referential character of *determinate* references, say, names and demonstratives. The first and rather forlorn sub-strategy, (A-1), is to

*equate*

    Something is a lion

with

    Leo is a lion or Nixon is a lion or Gibraltar is a lion or (perhaps) the number
    3 is a lion, or etc.

This sub-strategy, though not without its temptations, runs into familiar road-
blocks. The 'etc.' is doing a lot of unexplained work. As Ms. Anscombe has
pointed out, the 'etc.' (or the dots which may replace it) is not the 'etc.' of lazi-
ness. Yet when we reflect on the different ways in which 'something' and 'everything' refer indeterminately to all objects, we are bound to feel that 'or' and 'and'
have *something* to do with the distinction.

14.     The second and more lively sub-strategy under (A), (A-2), introduces the
theme of truth conditions for

    Something is a lion

and interprets the situation as follows:

    'Something is a lion' is true ≡ some statement which makes a determinate
    reference to an object and classifies it as a lion is true.

I formulate it in this way to stress its attempt to explain indeterminate reference
in terms of determinate reference. This sub-strategy has the advantage of not pre-
tending that we can actually come up with the list of determinate references which
would be necessary to yield something "equivalent' to the original statement, let
alone synonymous with it.

15.     But while (A-2) has this advantage, it has troubles of its own. Statements
are made in a language, and the resources of any natural language are always limited—certainly with respect to determinate referring expressions. One who pro-
pounds (A-2) will scarcely construe the phrase 'some statement which makes a
determinate reference to an object' as referring to statements containing one or

other of a list of such expressions in current usage. Such a proponent must rather rely on the fact that a language not only consists of more than the grammatical strings which are actually deployed at any one time (which is obvious), but also of more than the grammatical strings which are available for deployment. It also includes, in a sense difficult to define, the resources by which the language could be enriched through being extended in specific ways. It is this notion of the extendibility of a language which gives what plausibility it has to (A-2) as a strategy for explaining indeterminate reference terms of determinate reference.[1]

16.     But what is the alternative? It is, to my mind, a most puzzling one, though its puzzling aspects are quietly passed over; indeed, I would say swept under the rug by those who espouse it. For it amounts to nothing more nor less than the idea that the word 'something' has a connection, unmediated by determinate references, with all objects—and by 'connection', as will become evident, I mean a genuine relation[2] to be captured by psycho-linguistic theory.

17.     I have been discussing the issue in terms of the word 'something'. But its bite remains when we transpose it into the language of the logicians, where

Something is a tiger and is tame

becomes

$(\exists x)$ x is a tiger and x is tame.

The variable 'x' is said to range over objects. But it is not clear what it is for a variable to "range" over objects. Is there a "word-world" connection between variables and items in the extra-linguistic realm of stones and tigers? If so (and the answer must surely be 'yes') is this "ranging"—which is clearly the counterpart of the indeterminate reference of 'something'—to be explicated in terms of determinate reference or is it to be taken as a basic mode of reference?

---

[1] A more serious difficulty arises, however, when this strategy tries to take into account that the domain of objects includes real numbers. It is, perhaps, evident that all extensions of a language contain at most a denumerable infinity of determinate referring expressions. An assessment of this difficulty must await an explication of the sense in which numbers are objects.

[2] By 'genuine' relation I mean, roughly, descriptive relation. In this sense, neither 'or(p,q)' nor 'greater(9,7)' express relations. How, exactly, the distinction between 'descriptive' and its complement ('logical?') is to be drawn is part of the problem.

18.    I have no objection whatever to treating, as a logician might do, the concept of indeterminate reference as an unanalyzed concept in semantical theory. But the task of explicating it confronts the philosophical logician as a challenge which should not be ignored and will not go away.

19.    In formal semantics, one may, in a sense, explain the indeterminate reference of a statement, for example,

$(\exists x)$ x is a lion

which belongs to the object language of which one is "giving the semantics," by giving the statement's truth conditions in an appropriate metalanguage, thus

'$(\exists x)$ x is a lion' (in L) is true $\equiv$ $(\exists x)$ x satisfies 'x is a lion' (in L)

or, to solve certain formal problems

$(\exists s)$ s satisfies 'x is a lion' (in L)

where 's' ranges over infinite sequences of objects. But it leaps to the eyes that the problem of the nature of indeterminate reference has simply been transferred to the metalanguage. I don't say that this isn't where it belongs—indeed, sub-strategy (A-2) made a parallel move. But in giving the truth condition of

Something is a lion

in the metalanguage, it did so by referring to statements of determinate reference in the object language, rather than by simply adding an indeterminate reference to objects to the metalanguage. It at least *attempted* to come to grips with the problem. The above "explication" of indeterminate reference in terms of truth conditions simply postpones the problem.

20.    Even if one restricts the range of 'something' to individuals in Space and Time, the puzzle is acute. It becomes particularly obtrusive when the claim is made that the referential character of proper names can be explicated in terms of the referential character of descriptive phrases, the latter being traced, in turn, to the referential character of 'something'. According to an oversimplified form of this

strategy, 'Plato' would be construed as 'the student of Socrates and teacher of Aristotle' and this, in turn, with Russellian niceties, in terms of 'something is uniquely a student of Socrates and teacher of Aristotle'. Fully carried out, this move would involve reconstructing all proper names in terms of predicative counterparts as would be illustrated by construing 'Nixon' as

the Nixonizer

which, in turn, would be given a contextual analysis in terms of

something uniquely Nixonizes.

21.    As I have already pointed out, it would seem to be obvious that expressions with successful determinate reference are *connected* with the extra-linguistic world, thus 'Plato' with a Greek philosopher, and 'Nixon' with that man in the White House. On views of the kind we have just been considering, this connection is to be interpreted as a *focusing* of a connection between 'something' and objects in general or on a particular object by means of one or more predicates which pick it out. Determinate reference is the focusing of indeterminate reference. Quine tells us that variables of quantification are the "bearers of reference"—in traditional terms that 'something' is the bearer of reference. I am simply asking that this be taken seriously, which, as I see it, involves at least sketching an account of *how* "variables of quantification" hook up with the world.

22.    I pointed out above that 'ranges over' might be construed as an undefined term in semantical theory for the manner of hook-up. It might serve the purpose of a promissory note to be cashed in terms of a psycho-linguistic account of how language *as linguistic behavior* hooks up with the world. But then one would like *some* account of why psycho-linguistics would find it fruitful to focus the hook-up on a relation between objects and variables of quantification. Must one be satisfied with a Duhemian gambit to the effect that the apparatus of quantification is but the skeleton of a language-whole and that it is the language-whole which hooks up with the world by "confronting the tribunal of experience"? Can one say no more than that the "variables of quantification" hook up because the language-whole hooks up? Perhaps one can say that the language-whole hooks up because observation sentences hook-up. Clearly to say something illuminating about 'something', one

must say a lot.

23.    Notice that I am not objecting to the concept of indeterminate reference. Indeterminate reference can not be avoided—except, perhaps, by God, who has a name for each sparrow which falls. The problem, rather, is *how* the concept of such reference is to be explicated. Neither of the strategies we have considered dispenses with quantification. In both, the word 'some' was used in the explication of the indeterminate reference of 'something' in

Something is a lion.

In the first sub-strategy, it appeared in

*Some* statement which makes a determinate reference to an object and classifies it as a lion is true.

In the second, it appeared in

$(\exists x)$ x satisfies 'x is a lion'
and
$(\exists x)$ 'x is a lion' is true of x

which correspond, respectively, to

*Something* satisfies 'x is a lion'

and

'x is a lion' is true of *something*.

24.    Some philosophers have tended to overlook this problem, because in dealing with formalized languages, the resources of which are recursively specified by an effective procedure, they use a concept of reference which is not that of a connection between expressions and items in the world, though it is, in an interesting sense, parasitical upon it. This concept is defined in purely logical terms, thus

x refers to y (in L) $=_{df}$ x = 'New York' (in L) and y = New York or x = 'Chicago' (in L) and y = Chicago or x = 'Nixon' (in L) and y = Nixon ... .

Such a defined notion, as I pointed out in my essay for the Carnap volume[3] some twenty years ago, is useful in constructing a recursive account of the semantical properties of the expressions of the formalized language, but they no more explicate the concept of *reference* than

x is the Dutch uncle of y $=_{df}$ x = Mr. Jones and y = Tom or x = Mr. Smith and y = Dick or x = Mr. Roberts and y = Harry ...

explicates what it is to be a Dutch uncle.

25.　The puzzle of indeterminate reference becomes truly formidable when the concept of reference is extended to abstract objects, thus attributes, classes, classes of classes, numbers, propositions etc. How, one wants to know does the word 'something' hook up with them? Here, moreover, the tension is heightened by the fact that even the concept of *determinate* reference to an abstract entity is highly problematic.

26.　In the case of concreta there are signs that progress is being made in developing a theory of determinate reference. Attempts are being made at a causal theory of proper names which, if successful, would give the sort of focused or non-Duhemian account of reference adumbrated in paragraph 22 above. Thus, if indeterminate reference could be explicated in terms of determinate reference, the problem of reference in so far as it relates to non-abstract objects would be under control.

27.　But what of abstract objects, construed in the classical manner as irreducible to non-abstract objects? How in this case is determinate reference to be understood? If 'Socrates' refers to an ancient Greek philosopher by virtue of psycho-socio-linguistic connections, must there not be psycho-socio-linguistic connections between, for example, 'triangularity' and triangularity and 'mankind' and the class of men?

---

[3] "Empiricism and Abstract Entities," in *The Philosophy of Rudolf Carnap* (edited by Paul A. Schilpp), LaSalle, Illinois, 1963 [reprinted in EPH(94)].

28.    Notice that it won't do to grant the general point that the word 'triangularity' has a psycho-socio-linguistic connection with *something*, but claim that it is with triangular things, for triangularity is neither constituted by nor identical with any collection of triangular things, and could be referred to as readily if there were no triangular things.

29.    The classical Platonist was perfectly content to speak of real relations between Forms and persons. He was willing to use the languages of vision and of intercourse. Plato's Forms made themselves known to us by acting on our minds—and if the concept of a cause which does not change in the course of causing is a puzzling one, at least it was a serious attempt to deal with a serious problem. In Christian Neo-Platonism this causation became the agency of God, but the concept of the illumination of the mind was essentially the same. Platonists believed themselves aware of experiencing the Forms, but they also thought that the influence of the Forms, whether we were aware of it or not, was necessary to explain how we could think of the world as we do and how we could know mathematical, ethical, and metaphysical truths.

30.    Many philosophers who have an ontology which includes irreducible abstract objects have felt uncomfortable about the idea of a *causal* relation between these objects and persons. They have stressed, instead, the concept of awareness. We are "aware" of universals, classes, attributes and their ilk. Whether this "awareness" is construed as an "act," a "relation" or a "tie," it is presumably a matter-of-factual or non-logical connection which mediates between the abstract object and the causal chain which culminates in the abstract term which refers to that object. I suspect, however, that when the metaphors and mysteries with which the concept of "awareness" are shrouded become spelled out, something like the Platonic theme of causal efficacy will be found at the core. After all, traditional concepts of awareness, at least as recently as Moore, were based on the analogy of vision—and can vision be understood without causality?

31.    In my Carnap essay I made the point that a semantical theory which finds a genuine place for abstract entities as irreducible objects would have to recognize matter-of-factual relations between these entities and persons. Carnap denied this, of course, but his denial simply mobilized the strategy, to which attention has already been called, of defining a "relation" of "reference" in terms of disjunction, conjunction and identity. Thus, in the case of numbers we would have, already noted,

$$x \text{ designates-in-G } y \; =_{df} \; x = \text{ 'Eins' and } y = \text{ one or}$$
$$x = \text{ 'Zwei' and } y = \text{ two or}$$
$$\dots$$

But, as in the case of non-abstract objects, such a concept of "designates-in-L," defined by a listing, no more explicates the connection between number words and numbers, classically conceived as irreducible non-linguistic objects, than it explicates the connection between the word 'Chicago' and the windy city.

32.    Needless to say, the Duhemian strategy is lurking in the wings. Thus, suppose a platonist with respect to attributes and/or classes to be asked: "Must there not be matter-of-factual relations between abstract entities and human minds by virtue of which abstract singular terms acquire a hook-up with the world?" Might not our platonist reply: "It is our theory as a whole, including its logical apparatus and such sortal predicates as 'molecule', 'positron', 'attribute', 'proposition', 'class', 'class of classes', etc., which confronts the tribunal of experience. Our language hooks up with positrons and classes alike by virtue of the application of the theory to experience. It is only the will-o-the-wisp of the analytic-synthetic distinction which keep one from recognizing that 'class' and 'proposition' are in a continuum with 'current' and 'positron'. It is simply a matter of degrees of theoreticity, of remoteness from the occasion-sentences elicited by sensory stimulation."

33.    The following consideration, however, should generate a measure of skepticism with respect to this facile gambit. The theory-whole has specific things to say about the causal relations which connect micro-physical objects with the sensory stimulations which bombard the sensory surfaces of experimenters looking at bubble chambers and photographic plates. The theory explains *how* we are in touch with micro-physical objects.

34.    Thus, in addition to the Duhemian point that *expressions* for micro-physical particles acquire a hook-up with micro-physical particles by virtue of belonging to a theory which is applied as a whole, the theory offers a causal account of the *specifics* of the hook-up. This is not the case with such terms as 'number', 'class', 'attribute', and 'proposition'. This fact introduces a radical discontinuity into Quine's Continuum, one which has important consequences for the problem of abstract entities, for ontology and, above all, for the philosophy of mind.

## 2 THE QUEST FOR PROPERTIES

or

## WHEN IS A SORT NOT A SORT?

1.     Philosophers have a peculiar form of the Midas touch. Everything they touch becomes a puzzle, and eventually a problem. The concept of reference, and, particularly, of indeterminate reference is certainly no exception. I have touched it and, speaking for myself, at least, have found myself confronting the problem of how words and the world are related. I found it evident that in the case of ordinary objects, at least, determinate reference involves real relations between objects and the expressions which refer to them. But while I found this general thesis evident, I found nothing evident about what specifically these relations might be. Indeed, it has long been my conviction that this general thesis poses one of the key problems of philosophy and it is a recurring theme in my writings that only a thoroughly naturalistic philosophy of mind can solve it. One of my purposes in this volume is to clarify and elaborate this theme and to make my arguments more persuasive than they have thus far turned out to be.

2.     In addition to touching on the problem of indeterminate reference, which, in spite of its close connection with basic issues in ontology, has remained largely in the background, I also touched on the topic of determinate reference to abstract objects, though I pursued it just far enough to introduce my own perplexities. I shall return to the topic of abstract entities and how we refer to them in the concluding chapter. But before I do so, more remains to be said about the versatility of the word 'something'. The first chapter was entitled "In Praise of 'Something'" but the topic has barely been introduced.

I

3.       I shall make the central point without the elaborate dialectic with which I introduced and defended it some seventeen years ago in a previous essay in ontology.[1] It is to the effect that in ordinary language we can not only generalize from

Tom is tall
to
Something is tall

but also from

Jones is pale and Smith is also pale
to
Jones is *something* and Smith is also *it*

and from

Jones is a professor and Smith is also a professor
to
Jones is a *something* and Smith is also an *it*.

And even, though I shall not argue the point, from

If Jones comes, then there will be trouble
to
If *something,* then there will be trouble.

4.       Thus 'something' can be used in contexts in which it replaces an adjective, contexts in which it replaces a sortal and even contexts in which it replaces a sentence. It will be helpful for our purposes, however, to introduce a terminology in which the word 'something' is replaced by a number of expressions each of which contains an indication of the grammatical category of the determinate expressions

---

[1] "Grammar and Existence: A Preface to Ontology" (GE(37), reprinted in SPR(53)].

it is to replace. Thus, instead of

Jones is *something* and Smith is also *it*,

I will write

Jones is some*how* and Smith is also *it*
or
Jones is some*how* and Smith is that*how*.

Strictly speaking this is not an ideal choice, for

How is Jones?

would not normally be answered by

Jones is pale,

let alone

Jones is tall;

but I can think of nothing better, unless we go, as I once did, to the latinate 'some*quale*'.[2]

5.       Correspondingly, I shall use

Jones is a some*sort*

to express the above generalization from

Jones is a professor

and, using a terminology suggested by Arthur Prior,

---

[2] Chapter 8, paragraph 33 in SPR).

If some*that*, there will be trouble.

II

6.       I shall set the stage for the argument to come by pointing out that there is no surface reason to think that

Jones is some*how* and Smith is that*how*

makes an explicit ontological commitment. The first clause is a contrived paraphrase of

Jones is something

which does not have, at least on the surface, the form

Something is a K

or

There are Ks

which were our paradigms for ontological commitment.

7.       Notice that we must be careful not to split up the 'some*how*' and the 'that*how*' of our contrived statement into 'some how' and 'that how'. For this might tempt us to construe 'how' as a sortal, and hence to move from

Jones is some how and Smith is that how

to

There is a how such that Jones is it and Smith is it

and from this to

There are hows.

Perhaps further argument will lead us to the idea that there *are* hows, but we should not beg the question to begin with.

8.        I might also note, parenthetically, that there is a similar danger in reading 'something' as 'some thing'. To do so is to lay oneself open to the temptation to construe

> Something is a tiger

as

> Some thing is a tiger

and hence, implicitly, as

> Something is a thing and it is a tiger.

When made thus explicit it is obvious that something has gone wrong. The 'thing' of 'something' is not a sortal.[3]

III

9.        Having introduced specialized contrivances to play some of the roles of 'something', I shall leave them in the background until I have zeroed in on the puzzles they will help to clarify. In the meantime I shall use a mode of representation which makes use of the vocabulary of symbolic logic. Thus, for

> Jones is some*how* and Smith is that*how*,

I shall use

> ($\exists$f) Jones is f and Smith is f

or

> ($\exists$f) f(Jones) and f(Smith).

---

[3] This corresponds to the temptation to give an informal reading to '($\exists$x)x is a tiger' according to which it becomes 'There is a thing (or object) such that it is a tiger'. I called attention at length in "Grammar and Existence" to the *philosophical* (*not* computational) dangers lurking in informal readings of logical symbolisms.

10.     Looking at the latter representations we might be tempted to think of 'f' as a restricted variable ranging over a sub-domain of objects. To do so would be to assimilate these representations to the case in which instead of representing

Some crows are black

as

($\exists$x) x is a crow and x is black,

we are led by a single-minded interest in crows to use the variable 'c' to range over the more restricted universe which they constitute, generating

($\exists$c) c is black

as, in the case of numbers we might use

($\exists$n) n is divisible by 3

instead of

($\exists$x) x is a number and x is divisible by 3.

11.     Thus we might think that

($\exists$f) f(Jones)

is a quantificationally restricted form of

($\exists$x) x is an attribute and Jones has x

which latter would, on our assumptions, correspond to

There is an attribute such that Jones has it

and make an explicit ontological commitment to attributes.

12.     Notice that attributes in this sense would be abstract *objects* which are

"had" (or "exemplified") by concreta. Notice also that there would be a radical discrepancy between the surface logical form of the unquantified statement with which we began, i.e.

Jones is pale

and that of its quantified counterpart, i.e.

There is an attribute such that Jones *has* it.

13.     There is, of course, another explanation of how one might come to think that the symbolic representation involves attributes as abstract objects. Thus, one might reason that our quantified statement has the following truth condition:

'Jones is somehow' (in E) is true  ≡  There is an attribute such that the object named (in E) by 'Jones' *has* it

or, *logistice*,

'(∃f) Jones is f' (in E) is true  ≡  (∃x) x is an attribute and 'Jones has y' (in E) is true of x.

14.     But though these bi-conditionals are indeed true, it is not because truth conditions for

Jones is somehow.            (∃f) Jones is f.

*must* be given in these terms, but simply because for every statement of the form

Jones is thus-and-so.        Jones is f.

there is a corresponding statement—logically equivalent to it, but not *synonymous* with it—of the form

Jones has f-ness.

15.    Thus

Jones is somehow

although logically equivalent to

There is an attribute which Jones has

is not synonymous with it.

16.    Furthermore, a Fregean would claim that the above reasoning begs the question by assuming that truth conditions must be given in terms of *objects*. One can, indeed, be exclusively interested in *interpretations* of sentences in which the variables of quantification range over *objects*; and, indeed, one might so use the phrase 'truth on an interpretation' that it contains this stipulation. But it would seem, at least at first sight, open to one to distinguish between 'truth on an interpretation', thus construed, and 'truth' *period*. I have already availed myself of Carnap's Principle of Tolerance (a contemporary form of H.W.B. Joseph's plea for free-thinking in logistics) and claimed the right to use the full symbolic apparatus of quantification in connection with predicate variables, while rejecting, at least until additional considerations are brought to bear, the idea that this use *entails* an ontological commitment to attributes as *objects* which ordinary objects *have*.

IV

17.    At this point a Fregean might chime in with the claim that the variable 'f' ranges over *non-objects* (i.e. in his sense: concepts)—and propose as truth condition the following:

'($\exists$f) Jones is f' (in E) is true $\equiv$ ($\exists$f) 'Jones is $\varphi$' (in E) is true of f

by analogy with

'($\exists$x) x is pale' (in E) is true $\equiv$ ($\exists$x) '$\varphi$ is pale' (in E) is true of x.

18.    Or, to put it somewhat differently, he might revive strategy (A-2) which was applied in Chapter 1 to 'Something is a lion'. This strategy (called, in the case of formalized languages, the substitutional approach) would generate

'Jones is some*how*' (in E) is true  ≡  Some sentence (in E) consisting of a
                                        predicate and 'Jones is' is true.

19.    The former—or bolder—approach which takes 'f' to range over non-objects—one is tempted to say *hows*—does indeed seem to be close to making an explicit ontological commitment to these non-objects, though it is not exactly clear how it does it. For it won't do just to *say*, without argument, that

(∃f) Jones is f

can, for philosophical purposes, be paraphrased as

There is a non-object, f, such that Jones is f.

20.    Now the claim that there are non-objects which things *are* does not, of course, preclude the recognition that there are abstract objects (attributes) which things *have*. Indeed an essential part of Frege's own ontology is that to the non-objects we have been considering there correspond objects which are their "correlates."

21.    Thus, before discussing attributes as *objects* we must come to terms with the non-objects which Frege called concepts, but for which Geach has suggested the term 'property'.[4] (I shall use the term 'attribute' for non-Fregean abstract objects and the term 'property' for these putative Fregean non-objects.)

22.    It will be useful at this point to introduce a strategy which has its roots in *Principia Mathematica* but which has recently been purged of ambiguity and confusion and put to good use by Quine[5] and by Richard M. Martin[6]—the strategy of "virtual classes." Given a predicate or open sentence we can form a "virtual

[4] Peter Geach, "What There is," in *Aristotelian Society Supplementary Volume* XXV (1951).
[5] W. V. O. Quine, *Set Theory and its Logic,* Cambridge (Mass.), 1963.
[6] R. M. Martin, *Intension and Decision,* Prentice-Hall, 1963.

class abstract" which itself functions as a predicate; one which is logically equivalent to that from which it is formed. The important thing about virtual class
expressions, as Quine and Martin see it, is that while they are not *names* of the
*classes* corresponding to the predicates or open sentences with which one begins,
they have a syntax which permits them to be read as though they were class membership expressions. Thus, from the open sentence

x is red

one can form the abstract

/x: x is red/

which we prefix by '$\in$' (read 'is a(n)') to get

$\in$ /x: x is red/

which has as its primary reading 'is an x such that x is red'. Its secondary reading
(with which we shall not be concerned) would be 'is a member of the (virtual)
class of the xs such that x is red'.

23.     Thus, instead of

Tom is red,

we can say

Tom $\in$ /x: x is red/

or, provisionally,

Tom is an x such that x is red.

24.     Now it is important to note that although the predicate with which we began
is not a sortal, the abstract which is introduced is *treated as a sortal*. Quine and
Martin tacitly recognize this shift and indicate that if one prefers one may simply

use the abstract as a predicate by dropping the '∈' and prefixing the abstract to the relevant term, thus

/x: x is red/Tom,

but unless this is read in a way which echoes class talk, some of the magic is gone. Perhaps we should read it as

[an x such that x is red]Tom

where the use of brackets indicates that what they group together is functioning as a predicate.

25.     Clearly some attention should be paid to clarifying the exact sense in which a virtual class abstract functions as a sortal. The problem will recur.

V

26.     Before considering other applications of the strategy of virtual classes, a reflection on the concept of a variable is in order. It is important to distinguish, with Quine, between *variables* and *dummy constants*. The key difference is that variables are subject to quantification, whereas expressions containing dummy constants yield statements only when the latter are replaced with full-blooded constants. Thus, where 'f' plays the role of a variable, we can go from

Tom is f

to the statement

(∃f) Tom is f.

If, on the other hand, it is a dummy predicate, we can only form, by replacement, such a statement as, for example,

Tom is wise.

27.      There are locutions in ordinary language which seem to perform the role of dummy constants—for example, when children are taught grammar. I have in mind expressions like 'such and such', 'so and so', and, in certain contexts, their simpler cousins 'such' and 'so'.

28.      Thus if we think of the 'f' in

(x) fx ∨ ~fx

as a dummy constant we might read this formula as

Everything is either so or not so.

Although ordinary language has nothing that does the exact job of a variable, we could borrow its dummy constants and give them the role of variables, using them in informal readings of logical formulae. This I shall do in what follows.

29.      We are now in a position to use the technique of virtual classes in connection with open sentences containing unbound predicate variables. I move directly to an example which bears on our Fregean problem. Consider

(x) fx ∨ ~fx

where 'f' is a variable.

30.      As before, we construct the abstract, this time

/f: (x) fx ∨ ~fx/

and, playing to the hilt the game of virtual classes (this time, *in some sense*, of the second order), introduce 'ε' (read, as before, 'is a(n)') getting

ε /f: (x) fx ∨ ~fx/

which, for the moment we read

is an f such that everything is f or not f.

31.    Once again we have expanded our nominal resources. Just as before we acquired a new way of saying 'Tom is red', namely 'Tom $\in$ /x: x is red/', so we now have a new way of saying

Everything is red or not red

namely,

Red $\in$ /f: (x) fx $\vee$ ~fx/

or, informally,

Red is an f such that everything is f or not f.

32.    It is essential to note that although 'red' is serving here (at least in appearance) as the subject of a statement of the form

--- is a K,

it is not a singular term, but though it is not actually functioning in this context as a predicate, has retained its predicative character. Thus there would be no equivocation in the use of 'red' were we to say

This book is red *and* red $\in$ /f: (x) fx $\vee$ ~fx/.

33.    By writing the more complex

red $\in$ /f: (x) fx $\vee$ ~fx/

instead of

(x) redx $\vee$ ~redx,

we have, so to speak, taken the two occurrences of 'red' out of the latter statement, leaving its logical skeleton behind, and combined them into one prefixed occurrence—all in such a way as to make, in effect, the same statement.

34.     If we use our other option, to drop the 'ε' and to treat the abstract as though it were a predicate, then

/f: (x) fx ∨ ~fx/red,

in the language of virtual classes, i.e. giving the abstract a sortal ring, becomes

[an f such that (x) fx ∨ ~fx]red.

35.     We now have the nominal resources by means of which to introduce the term 'property' in a way which, at least at first sight, seems to capture the meaning of Frege's 'concept'. For by preserving the predicative character of predicate expressions, as noted in paragraph 33, our strategy enables us, at least in appearance, to do justice to the idea that a concept is not an object, not an attribute which objects *have*; it is, as Geach and Dummett insist,

Something which everything *is* or *is not*.

36.     We simply equate

red is a property

with

red ∈ /f: (x) fx ∨ ~fx/
i. e.,
red is an f such that (x) fx ∨ ~fx.

37.     If, now, we generalize from

red is a property

in accordance with our *tolerated* treatment of quantification, we get

(∃f) f is a property
(∃f) f is a concept

which it feels comfortable to read as

There are properties
There are concepts.

## VI

38.     If the above line of reasoning could be defended, it would have two virtues:

(1)     It would show how a Fregean could make an explicit ontological commitment to concepts or properties, items which things *are* rather than *have*.

(2)     It would get Frege off a notorious hook. He was puzzled about how one could say that

red is a concept

for 'red' seems to function here as a singular term or "name" and hence to stand for an object. According to the above line of thought, the latter statement would only superficially have the form

[object] is a [non-object].

39.     What I have done is to reconstruct, by a judicious combination of the formalism of virtual classes with the informal readings which are used to back up the description of the formalism as a theory of virtual classes, the line of thought which, as I see it, is lurking in Geach's and Dummett's neo-Fregean semantics, and, in particular, their explanation of why no paradox is involved in such statements as

Red is a concept (or a property)

and why there is no problem about making explicit ontological commitment to concepts or properties.

40.   Of course, on the classical account of quantification, the minute we treat 'red' in

red is a property

as a suitable place for quantification, we have introduced reference to *objects*. Accordingly,

(∃f) f is a property

is to be construed as an explicit commitment to abstract objects, i.e., to *attributes*. It would be true if and only if

There is an object such that everything either *has* it or *doesn't have* it.

41.   The immediate moral is that classical quantification theory plays a key role in contemporary ontology and hence requires a no-holds-barred scrutiny to determine whether its hands are clean—i.e. that the questions at stake are not, in the last analysis, being begged.

## VII

42.   Well, does this ingenious strategy work? Only, of course, if

(a) it is entitled to

(∃f) f is a property

and

(b) it is entitled to paraphrase the latter as

There are properties.

Of these, the former is crucial, for once it is granted the latter may seem to follow as a matter of course. Yet even here one must be careful.

43.     I have already pointed out that it would be a howler to read

$(\exists f)$ f is a property

as

Somehow is a property,

then break up 'somehow' into 'some how' and get

Some how is a property,

and reason, by analogy with,

Some dog is an animal
Therefore, there are animals

that

Some how is a property
Therefore, there are properties.

I have already pointed out that the 'how' in 'somehow' is not a sortal. The word is a unity and its appearance of composition springs from the fact that it belongs with other expressions containing 'how' in an apparatus of cross-reference. Thus,

Jones is somehow and Smith is that*how*
Jones is somehow and Smith is also *it.*

Compare

Something is red and it/thatthing is also square.

44.    But perhaps one can go directly from

(∃f) f is a property

to

There are properties

without this mediating confusion. This is where the crucial question arises: is our neo-Fregean entitled to the sortal context

Red is a property?

45.    I have already suggested that the reading of the first order abstract

/x: x is red/

as a sortal is gratuitous and springs from the temptation to treat 'x' itself as a sortal, as when one reads

(∃x) x is a lion

as

There is an x such that x is a lion.

Compare

There is an object, x, such that it is a lion.

46.    It would be of a piece with this to read the above abstract as

An x such that x is red

47.    This is reinforced by the fact that the reading

x such that x is red

won't do, for this would turn it into an open sentence rather than a predicate constant. The reading must in some way indicate that the variable, 'x', is bound. I suggest that we invent the expression 'athing' on the analogy of 'something', and read the abstract as

/athing such that it is red/.

*Not*, it should be emphasized,

/a thing such that it is red/

for this would create the illusion of a sortal and make it seem appropriate to introduce '∈' and construct such sentences as

Tom ∈ /x: x is red/

and read them as though they had the form

x is a K.

48.    With all this in mind, let us return to second level abstracts and, in particular, to the sentence

/f: (x) fx ∨ ~fx/red

which was supposed to reconstruct

Red is a property.

As a parallel to a point made in connection with first level abstracts, the above abstract would not be read

An f such that everything is f or not f,

but rather (with 'ahow' as the analogue of 'athing')

Ahow such that everything is it or not it
Ahow such that everything is thathow or not thathow.

49.     Only by constant vigilance can we avoid the temptation to read the abstract
in such a way as to give it the surface grammar of a sortal. I have deliberately highlighted this temptation in the above contrived reading which constantly threatens
to turn into

A how such that everything is that how or not that how

and thus, by a mistake which is rooted in firmly entrenched habits of reading quantified statements,

There is an x such that...
There is an f such that...,

commit the same mistake as that involved in the slide

Somehow is a property
Some how is a property
There are properties

or, *logistice,*

($\exists$f) f is a property.

50.     The sham sortal must be dropped. This, however, does not destroy the
usefulness of the 'virtual class' notation. It simply cuts off its supposed link with
ontological commitment. Thus, while

/f: (x) fx $\lor$ ~fx/red
/ahow such that everything is thathow or not thathow/red

is not a sortal statement, we can still introduce a philosophically interesting abbre-
viation for the abstract even though it is only in the *broadest* of senses a predicate

concatenated with 'red'. Thus instead of

Red is a property

we could write

Attributive red.

If one sneaks in a copula on the ground that it is appropriate wherever "predi-cation" is found, thus

Red is attributive,

one might find oneself on the way to a metaphysics of the Analogy of Being. But with caution the use of the copula can be treated as a useful grammatical surface structure.

51.    Above all, it must be remembered that

Attributive red

is, by stipulation, logically equivalent to

Everything is red or not red.

Its primary interest lies in the fact that in a sense it provides a way of *saying* something which is only *shown* by the latter, namely that 'red' has a certain logical form.

52.    Appealing as before, to the principle of tolerance and the spirit of free-thinking in logistics, we can generalize from

Attributive red

to

($\exists$f) attributive f.

But this would not put us within shooting distance of

There are attributive entities

unless we felt entitled to read

($\exists$f) attributive f

as

Some entity, f, is attributive

or

There is an entity, f, which is attributive

which would amount to nothing less than an abandonment of all our painstakingly constructed clarifications; a mad rush over the verbal bridges which tie classical quantification theory so closely to objects. And, in any case, if we do make this move, we won't end up with Geach's and Dummett's properties or Frege's concepts, but rather with *objects*, i.e., with attributes as abstract objects which concreta *have* or *exemplify*, rather than *non-objects* which they *are*.

## VIII

53.     Similar considerations emerge when we test neo-Fregean theory against our provisional requirements for a naturalistic theory of reference. It will be remembered that according to these requirements an appropriate statement of reference for predicative expressions, has, at least in first approximation, the form illustrated by

'Red' refers to red things
'Man' refers to men

which are to be construed as in some sense implying a real connection between predicative expressions and things in the world. I shall assume, in what follows, that statements of reference not merely imply "in some sense" such a connection, but themselves assert it to obtain.

54.     The second of the above statements, then, asserts a (presumably complex) connection to obtain between the word 'man' (or sentences containing the word

'man') and persons. I shall subsequently be concerned with what the connection might be, but the point I wish to make now doesn't hinge on the specifics of a theory of reference.

55.     Now a statement to the effect that the word 'man' is connected with men is presumably exponible in terms of tokens of the word 'man'. That is, the word ' 'man' ' which occurs as the subject of a singular sentence, for example,

'man' is a noun,

is functioning as what I have called a distributive singular term.[7] The sentence in question can be paraphrased as

a 'man' is a noun

and is to be construed as equivalent to

'Man's are nouns.

Thus we are considering such statements as

'red's refer to red things
'man's refer to men.

56.     Since it is an essential part of Frege's theory that what is referred to by a predicate is not an object, a Fregean is confronted by the problem of interpreting the role of the expression which follows the words 'refers to' in a statement of predicate reference. He clearly wants to be able to reason somewhat as follows:

Tom is a man
'Man' refers to ---
Tom is a [what 'man' refers to]
Tom is a ---.

---

[7]"Abstract Entities," (AE), reprinted in PPME.

57.    He would like to flesh this out as follows

Tom is a man
'Man' refers to man
Tom is a [what 'man' refers to]
Tom is a man.

58.    Notice that instead of

'Man' refers to men

we find

'Man' refers to man.

Thus it might seem that our Fregean is committed to the idea that the extra-linguistic term of the reference relation is the entity *man*, and hence that this entity is an object. For "genuine relations," as we have called them, hold between objects.

59.    It is important, therefore, for our Fregean to see that he does not have to insist on the form

'Man' refers to man

in order to be able to extract a predicative expression from the right hand side of a statement of reference.

60.    Consider the following statement, which will provide the necessary clue,

Bees live in hives

and consider the following reasoning

(1) Bees live in hives
(2) Tom lives in a hive
(3) What bees live in is hives

(4) Tom lives in what bees live in.

Obviously there is something to this line of thought, but its structure needs to be made more explicit.

61.     We proceed as follows:

(x)(x is a bee ⊃ (∃y) y is a hive and x lives in y)
Tom lives in a hive.

We now introduce the abstract

/K: (x)(x is a bee ⊃ (∃y) y is a K and x lives in y)/

which we read as

A sort such that for every bee something is a that sort such that the former lives in the latter

and, to reconstruct the third step in the above argument, concatenate this abstract with 'hive' to form the sentence

/K: (x)(x is a bee ⊃ (∃y) y is a K and x lives in y)/hive

which we read

Hive is a sort such that for every bee something is a that sort such that the former lives in the latter.

This sentence has the form

$$\varphi(f)$$

where 'φ' represents the abstract and 'f' represents 'hive'. It can be called a second level predication, but must be carefully distinguished from

$\varphi$(f-ness)

where 'f-ness' is the singular term, corresponding to the predicate 'f', which putatively refers to the abstract *object* (attribute) f-ness.[8]

62.     We next conjoin the above result with 'Tom lives in a hive', getting

/K: (x)(x is a bee $\supset$ ($\exists$y) y is a K and x lives in y)/hive *and* Tom lives in a hive.

By E-quantification on 'hive' we get

($\exists$K')(/K: (x)(x is a bee $\supset$ ($\exists$y) y is a K and x lives in y)/K'
*and* Tom lives in a K')

which is the reconstruction of the fourth step of the reasoning we are considering. We read it as

Somesort$_2$ is asort$_1$ such that every bee lives in a thatsort$_1$ and Tom lives in a thatsort$_2$

or, coming closer to the desired surface grammar,

Tom lives in somesort and thatsort is such that bees live in *them*.

63.     To apply this strategy to

'Man' refers to man

we must find a context having a quantificational structure which corresponds to

(x)(x is a bee $\supset$ ($\exists$y) y is a hive and x lives in y).

Making use of the plausible idea that 'man' refers to man by virtue of referring to

---

[8]Note, for future reference, that on elementarist principles '$\varphi$(f)' is to be construed as contextually definable in terms of '(x) fx $\supset$ $\varphi$x', in which occurs as a predicate of individuals.

each and every man, we come up with

$(x)(y)(x$ is a 'man' and $y$ is a man $\supset x$ refers to $y)$;

we form the abstract

$/K: (x)(y)(x$ is 'man' and $y$ is a $K \supset x$ refers to $y)/$

and then the sentence

$/K: (x)(y)(x$ is 'man' and $y$ is a $K \supset x$ refers to $y)/$man

or, telescoping steps,

$/K:$ 'man' refers to $Ks/$man
Man is asort such that 'man' refers to them.

Notice that the occurrence of 'man' with which this last sentence begins preserves its predicative character. Thus we can go from

Tom is a man

to

Tom is a man and man is asort such that 'man' refers to them

without equivocation.

64.        Finally we get

$(\exists K')(Tom$ is a $K'$ and $/K:$ 'man' refers to $Ks/K')$
Tom is somesort and thatsort is asort such that 'man' refers to them

which enables us to preserve the spirit of

Tom is [what 'man' refers to]

while insisting that

'Man' refers to men.

65.     Now the interest of all this maneuvering lies in the fact that neo-Fregeans like Geach and Dummett wish to explain properties (or, concepts) not only as

   what everything is or isn't

which we have already explored, but as

   what is referred to by predicates.

Thus,

   Man is a [what is referred to by predicates]
   Man is a property

(notice the 'a' which has crept in). For the above strategy can take us to

   /K: a predicate refers to Ks/man
   Man is a sort such that a predicate refers to them.

But, as before, to get from there to

   Man is a property (or concept),

we must interpret

   /K: a predicate refers to Ks/

as a sortal—and this there is no way to do. In the case of first order abstracts we could choose between the statement forms

   /x: x is red/Tom
and

Tom ∈ /x: x is red/

because '∈' (read 'is a(n)') is properly preceded by a singular term and by a singular term only. This elementary consideration is violated by

hive ∈ /K: (x)(x is a bee ⊃ (∃y) y is a K and x lives in y)/

if 'hive' is to retain its predicative character and not tacitly turned into 'hivehood'.
66.     We have been working with the sortal 'man', and our abstract does *contain* the grammatical role of sortals. It has the form

/K: a predicate refers to Ks/

which we have read

asort such that ... .

The temptation is strong indeed to treat this abstract as a sortal. But 'asort such that...' is *not* a sortal, and, in particular,

Man is asort such that ...

should not, if the considerations I have advanced in the course of this chapter are sound, be read

Man is a sort such that ...

for reasons which I have already noted on a number of occasions.
67.     Thus, once again, although we can agree that the abstract can be used to define a philosophically interesting expression, thus

attribute

and generate

attributive man

or, even,

Man (is) attributive,

only by mistake can one believe that the verbal bridges we have built bring us to an ontological commitment to "properties."

# 3  THE IMPORTANCE OF BEING DISPENSABLE

I

1.      In this chapter I shall argue, in accordance with the strategy outlined in chapter 1, that of course there are such abstract objects as attributes. I shall go on to develop a theory as to just what sort of objects they are. I shall, however, as you might expect, go on to argue that although there are attributes, there *really* are no attributes. It will be remembered that the qualification 'really' indicates that a philosophical point is being made, for in the *ordinary* sense of 'really', of course, there really are attributes.

2.      This argument will go hand in hand with a theory of predication which will strengthen the bite of the claim that although there are attributes, there *really* are no attributes. And this in turn will lay the groundwork for a theory of reference or, as I will also say, representation, which can claim to be the very foundation of a naturalistic ontology.

3.      I shall be approaching the questions raised in the first chapter from a somewhat different perspective. Thus, although the topic with which I begin is directly relevant to the general topic of the relation between language and the world, it focuses on a different aspect of language. In the first chapter I was concerned with the problem of *reference to objects* and raised the question of how expressions which *refer* to objects are, so to speak, hooked up with the objects (concrete or abstract) to which they refer.

4.      I now turn my attention to predicates, and while I have already had something to say about them in the second chapter, my concern was primarily with neo-Fregean attempts to show that taking the distinctive role of predicates seriously leads directly to an ontological commitment to a domain of predicative entities—

entities which are not objects and which are referred to by predicates. I shall have more to say on this topic at a later stage in the argument. For the moment I shall simply stress that one of the key merits of Frege's philosophy of language was this stress on the distinctive role of predicates, with respect to which they contrast with names, i.e., expressions referring to objects.

5.     That nominalistically inclined philosophers must agree with Frege that the role of predicates is distinctive is clear. They must, however, come up with a satisfactory account of what it is and to do so they must start from scratch, for once Frege's account is laid aside, as it must be if the argument of the last chapter is sound, no systematically developed alternative exists. Perhaps the best way of doing this is by rehearsing some of the basic dialectical moves which have been made in connection with predication.

6.     Thus, consider the two statements

    a is red
    a is green

where 'a' refers to an object which is, in point of fact, red. It is obvious that the words 'red' and 'green' contribute *something* to the meanings of these two sentences. Furthermore, it is equally obvious that there must be *something* in the extra-linguistic domain which corresponds to this contribution and helps account for the fact that the first of these statements is true, the second false. I say that these things are *obvious*, but they are also puzzling, as is made manifest by the use of the equally problematic words 'meaning' and 'true'—and, of course, of the word 'something'.

7.     Realism[1] in the broadest sense might be characterized as the above theses, which, since they are obvious, might be thought to be non-controversial. In philosophy, however, the bitterest controversies often center around the obvious. And without pressing at this time the words 'meaning' and 'true'—which will be engaging us soon enough—we can get the key dialectical moves underway by noticing that the thesis that "there must be *something* in the extra-linguistic domain which accounts for the fact that the first of the above statements is true,

---

[1] I use the term in the traditional sense in which it pertains to the problem of universals—conceptual realism as contrasted with realism in the theory of perception.

the second false," suggests, in the light of the versatility of 'something', the possibility of *three* general forms of "realism": (a) that which is willing to split up 'something' into 'some' and 'thing' and claim that what makes

a is red

true and

a is green

false is the presence of a connection between *a* and a 'thing' or *object* of a special kind (a universal or attribute) which is referred to by the word 'red', and the absence of such a connection between *a* and the object referred to by the word 'green'.

8.      (b) A second form of realism would be that which, while willing to split 'something' into 'some' and 'thing' and while advancing the same general formula, denies that either 'red' or 'green' refers to an object. This would be a realism, if etymology will forgive me, of non-things (*un-dinge*).

9.      Both of these first two forms of realism can be called "entitative," because each of them construes the truth of 'a is red' in terms of a connection between *a* and an *entity,* object or a non-object, which is referred to by the grammatical predicate.

10.      Obviously the third general form of realism will be a cagey form, which, while it agrees with the obvious, yet refuses to break up 'something' into 'some thing' and refuses to explain the truth of 'a is red' in terms of an entity which is referred to by 'red'. It is realism in this third sense which I propose to defend.

11.      Now for the dialectic. As good a place as any to begin with is Russell's classical argument for universals in *The Problems of Philosophy*. Since almost everybody cuts their teeth on it and uses it in their classroom, I can be brief and paraphrase freely. Russell argues that even the simplest sentence which is capable of truth or falsity must consist of more than expressions for particulars. It must also contain expressions which are not names of particulars, for example 'white' or 'to the north of'. Even if a tempting line of thought suggests that we can dispense with 'white', it would simply replace it by another expression which is equally not a name of a particular, i.e., 'resembles'. Since there are difficulties

about dispensing with 'white', we might as well reconcile ourselves to 'white' as well as 'resembles'.

12.     Well, suppose that Russell is right and that we do need such words. Grammatically they are predicates. He has *not* shown that we need abstract singular terms. 'White', yes, but not 'whiteness'. 'Resembles', yes, but not 'resemblance'. We need expressions which are not names of particulars. Do we need expressions which are names of non-particulars? Russell takes it for granted that the answer is "yes." Two considerations are obviously foremost in his mind. One is the general thesis of realism in the sense in which it expresses an obvious truth. The other is the fact that there actually are abstract singular terms in everyday use which are surely (a) meaningful, (b) *look* like names and (c) do not name particulars. Some of them are formed from predicative expressions by the use of such suffices as '-ity', '-hood', '-ness', '-dom', and, in Warren G. Harding's idiolect, '-cy'. Where an expression thus formed isn't at hand, we can always form an equivalent by using the gerundive form of the copula to form a substantive expression, thus

'(the attribute of) being ten feet tall'.

13.     What then would be the relation of the meaning of a predicate to that of the correlated abstract singular term? A number of sophisticated moves are obviously available, but it will be best to look first at the most simple, for that is how the traditional dialectic continues. Though simple, however, it can be, and has been, elaborated and defended in highly sophisticated ways.

14.     This ostensibly simple move argues that the difference between predicates and abstract singular terms is a superficial one. However the grammatical duplication is to be accounted for, it is, in principle, otiose.

15.     I shall speed up the dialectic by moving directly to *Principia* notation. I would certainly not claim that this notation—with its orientation towards mathematics—is adequate to express fully the logical form of even the simplest empirical statement. But it does capture *some* of it—one is tempted to say its skeleton—and much recent ontology has made full use of the fact. Thus, since the stage of the dialectic we are tuned in on is not concerned with time or tense, it has seemed appropriate to drop the copula and write 'a is red' as

red a.

16.     To switch examples, the move we are considering finds the difference between

> triangular a

and

> triangularity a

to be a purely superficial one, which does not reflect a significant semantical distinction. Indeed the second formulation is taken to be a more accurate portrayal of the semantical content of the assertion.

17.     If we turn our attention to relations, we are ready for a watershed in the dialectic—Bradley's puzzle about relations. Consider

> (1) Rab

where 'a' and 'b' are dummy names of particulars and 'R' is to be construed as 'R-hood', the dummy name of a relation. Bradley argued, in effect, that in order for (1) to be true, the items a, b, and R (R-hood) must be related. The mere collection

> a, b, R

is not a fact, and if 'Rab' simply stood for a collection, it would be a collection of expressions and not a statement. But if a, b, and R *are* related, then there must be a fact-making relation, R', which relates them. And if (1) is to be true, and more than a mere list of symbols, it must affirm that this relation obtains. To do so, it must refer to this relation. Since it does not do so explicitly, it must do so implicitly. (Presumably it does so by expressing an act of the understanding in which what is implicit *linguistically* is explicit *in thought*.) When the above commitment is made linguistically explicit, therefore, (1) would transform into

> (2) R' Rab

where 'R'' stands for R'-hood, the other symbols being interpreted as before. But it is clear that parity of reasoning would lead us quickly to the conclusion that (2) in its turn makes a commitment which, when made linguistically explicit, transforms it into

(3) R'' R' Rab

and so *ad infinitum*.

18.     Now when, in 1918, Russell was hit by Bradley's paradox many, many years after he first encountered it—a long double take—he resolved it in the following familiar way. He argued that 'Rab' expresses that a and b *stand in* R, not by covertly naming the relation of *standing in* but by itself being a relational pattern. Russell owed this counter to Wittgenstein, though he was not as clear about it as he might have been, and, indeed, as we shall see, misapplied Wittgenstein's strategy. If we echo the latter's well known thesis (*Tractatus,* 3.1432) in the context of the problem as Russell saw it, it becomes

> We say that a, b stand in R by placing the expressions 'a', 'b' and 'R' in a certain conventional triadic relation.

19.     Notice that this way of putting it has a certain paradoxical aspect which would have warmed Bradley's heart. For in the very process of telling us that we say that a, b stand in R by relating the *three* expressions 'a', 'b' and 'R', it implies that we can say the *same* thing by relating the four expressions 'a', 'b', 'R' and 'stand in'. If the same thing is said by 'Rab' and 'a, b stand in R', doesn't that amount to the idea that 'stand in' is "implicit in" 'Rab', in which case the regress is off and running.

20.     The name model for the constituents of basic sentences thus threatens to lead us back into the mire. Is there any way of preserving its essential claim, but avoiding this danger, by making minimal concessions to the view that basic sentences consist of non-names as well as names? The answer is 'yes'. But to see how this minimum concession can be made, it is first necessary to *increase the pressure* by formulating the above principle as follows:

> We can *only* say that a, b stand in R by placing the names 'a', 'b' and 'R' in a certain conventional triadic relation.

Obviously the only way to resolve the internal tension of this principle is by claiming that *both*

(1) Rab

and

(2) a, b stand in R

consist of the names 'a', 'b' and 'R' placed in different conventional *triadic* relations. To do this, we must interpret the syntactical form of (2) as a matter of the two names of particulars ('a', 'b') and the name of the relation ('R') as having a 'stand in' between them. From the standpoint of logical syntax, that is to say, both (1) and (2) would have the form

A triadic relation obtains between (tokens of) 'a', 'b' and 'R'.

21.     From this it would follow that in (2) 'stand in' is functioning in a radically different way than the other expressions. It is not a disguised name as are, according to this form of realism, ordinary predicates, but rather what might be called an *auxiliary symbol*. Furthermore, it is *dispensable*, for (1) and (2) have exactly the same meaning as far as their connection with the world is concerned. In *this* sense they say exactly the same thing; and, this being the case, we can say either

(1) and (2) both say that Rab

or

(1) and (2) both say that a, b stand in R.

22.     One more example of this realistic strategy and we will be in a position to draw certain morals. Consider

Triangular a.

According to the strong, or reifying, realism we are considering, this is only superficially different from

Triangularity a

and we are to construe the logical form of the latter in terms of the principle

> We can *only* say that a exemplifies f-ness by placing the name 'f-ness' and 'a' in a conventional dyadic relation.

23.     The internal tension in this principle is then resolved by claiming that

> (3) Triangularity a

and

> (4) a exemplifies triangularity

have the same syntactical form. Each consists of the names 'a' and 'triangularity' placed in a certain dyadic relation. In (3) the relation is simply that of linear concatenation with the abstract singular term to the left. In (4) it is a matter of the 'a' to the left and the 'triangularity' to the right having an 'exemplifies' between them. As in the case of 'stands in', 'exemplifies' is not a disguised name (as 'triangular' is construed to be), but rather an *auxiliary symbol*. It too is *dispensable*, for (3) and (4) have exactly the same meaning as far as their connection with the world is concerned. In *this* sense they say exactly the same thing, and we can put this accordingly either as

> (3) and (4) both say that triangularity a

or

> (3) and (4) both say that a exemplifies triangularity.

24.     Since instead of saying

> a, b stand in R

we could have said

> a, b exemplify R,

we can put the philosophical upshot of this entire realistic strategy in terms of a thesis about exemplification.

> Exemplification is a *tie* and not a relation. It can *only* be expressed by placing the name of the universal and the appropriate number of names of particulars, n, in a conventional $(n + 1)$-adic relation.

25.     It will not have escaped the knowledgeable reader that the views I have been describing are essentially those of that neo-Meinongian, Gustav Bergmann, one of the most coherent, drive down the road to the bitter end, ontological realists in the world today. It is amazing to see how the Metaphysics of Logical Positivism can proliferate in a short 25 years.

26.     Now there are obviously a number of puzzling things about this thesis. In the first place, it insists that exemplification can not be named. Yet 'exemplification' *looks* as much like a name as does 'juxtaposition', which, according to this thesis, *is* a name. Thus

> Juxtaposed a, b

is only superfically different on the view we are examining from

> Juxtaposition a, b

where 'juxtaposition' is the *name* of a relation. We would, therefore, like some story about why

> a exemplifies f-ness

isn't only superficially different from

> Exemplification a, f-ness

where 'exemplification' is the name of the relation of exemplification.

27.     No such story, however, is forthcoming. Yet this is not sufficient to discredit the strategy, and, indeed, the concept of a tie between objects (particulars and universals) which can only be expressed by placing the names of these objects

in a conventional n-adic configuration *does* break the Bradley regress.

28.    It is my purpose to argue that the above *strategy* is not only correct, but is the most basic of three essential elements in a sound theory of language as a representational system, in other words, a sound theory of meaning and truth. Notice that I said that the *strategy* is correct, because, I shall now argue that though correct, it was *misapplied*. It begins with too rich an ontology. As we shall see, it walks on semantic stilts.

29.    I shall introduce what I take to be the correct application of this strategy by asking the following question.

> Is it possible to apply this strategy while refusing to treat ordinary predicates as disguised *names* of abstract objects—or, for that matter, as referring to Fregean non-objects?

I submit that the answer is 'yes'. Thus we no longer treat PMese

Triangular a

as only superficially different from

Triangularity a,

but take its surface character as involving a non-name (the predicate 'triangular') at its face value. Similarly with relational statements. We no longer treat

Juxtaposed a, b

as only superficially different from

Juxtaposition a, b

but take the predicate 'juxtaposed' at its face value as a non-name. Treating, as before, such expressions as 'a', 'b', etc. as dummy names of non-abstract objects, without as yet scrutinizing what it is to be a name, we return to Wittgenstein's insight, this time giving it its proper application. I move directly to the formulation which forces the solution.

> We can *only* say that aRb by placing the names 'a' and 'b' in a certain conventional dyadic relation.

The 'only' is implicit in the *Tractatus,* but is demanded by Wittgenstein's theory of logical form.

30.    Consider, now

> (5)  a larger-than b

> (6)  $_b^a$.

From the standpoint of the above principle there might be a dialect of English in which (6) was used to say exactly what is said by (5). That is to say, these two expressions would have, to the sharpened eye, the same syntactical form, and the same connections with extra-linguistic reality.

31.    Notice that this time it is ordinary predicates which are interpreted as *auxiliary expressions*. Thus, in (5) by using the auxiliary expression 'larger than', we would have brought it about that the names 'a' and 'b' stand in the dyadic relation of having a 'larger-than' between them. In (6), on the other hand, the names 'a' and 'b' have been placed in the dyadic relation without the use of an auxiliary symbol.

32.    Clearly the dialect (I have called it Jumblese, the language I ascribe to the Jumblies of Edward Lear's nonsense poem) would be most awkward. It would be difficult to contrive an adequate system of patterns and styles with which to make sentences out of expressions referring to objects. It is much simpler to use auxiliary symbols and linear concatenation to get this variety in a manageable (if philosophically unperspicuous) way.

33.    Now you will miss the philosophical significance of this strategy if, as do most who encounter it, you say to yourself

> I suppose we *could* use ' $_b^a$ ' to say that a is larger than b

as you might say to yourself

I suppose we *could* refer to the future in soprano, the present in tenor, and the past in basso profundo

and add that this is a nice point to have made, but why run it into the ground. But the *possibility* of using '$\frac{a}{b}$' to say that a is larger than b is the trivial aspect of the thesis. The important aspect is the claim that

We can *only* say that a is larger than b by placing the names 'a' and 'b' in a (conventional) dyadic relation.

For it is *this* which is the foundation of a correct account of meaning and truth.
34.      Thus, one who is simply struck by the fact that we *could* use '$\frac{a}{b}$' to say that a is larger than b will be tempted to look for some aspect of

$$\frac{a}{b}$$

*which is doing the job done in*

a larger than b

by 'larger than': for example, "the *fact* that 'a' is above 'b'," of " 'a's *being above* 'b'." It is absolutely crucial to appreciate that *nothing in* (6), or *about* (6), is doing the job done in (5) by 'larger than'. Many philosophers have stared this point in the face and missed it, thus failing to grasp its significance.
35.      Obviously the fact that 'a' is above 'b' is essential to the semantical role (6) is playing. But that fact does not do the job done by 'larger than'. Rather it does the job done in the case of (5) by the fact that 'a' and 'b' have a 'larger than' between them. Let me repeat: *Nothing in (6), or about (6), is doing the job done by 'larger than'.*
36.      This is no mere quibbling, as should become clear when one realizes that the 'larger than' in (5) is an *object*, a linguistic inscription, *and not a fact. Indeed, Wittgenstein's own failure to appreciate the full significance of his analysis can be traced to his ontology of facts.*
37.      The above amounts to the claim that not only are predicative *expressions* dispensable, but the very *function* performed by predicates is dispensable. This,

if true, would strike a blow at the very heart of Frege's semantics. Let me therefore hasten to add, to forestall a serious misunderstanding, that I am applying Wittgenstein's strategy—as he did—only to empirical or matter-of-factual predicates, including those of theoretical science.

38.     Thus the term 'predicate' is often used in the broad sense in which any "open sentence" is characterized as a "predicative context." It is important, therefore, to see that when I say that *the very function of predicates is dispensable,* I am not making a claim which is absurd on the face of it. It may, in the last analysis, be absurd—in the last analysis, philosophical error always is—but its absurdity will have to be shown dialectically, by philosophical argument, not by pointing.

39.     From the perspective I have been developing, Frege had two insights about concept words of the kind corresponding to the predicates I have been discussing: (a) they are not names of objects; (b) predicates contribute in a unique way to the semantical role of the statements in which they occur. His mistake was to assimilate that role to the general category of reference, a mistake which, with (b), led inexorably to the view that predicates *refer to non-objects.*

40.     We are also able to locate an insight of Quine's. He has argued, in "On What There Is" and other places, that predicates are syncategorematic expressions, contributing to the meaning of sentences without having reference. They present the "ideology" of a language rather than its ontology. They are said to be "true of" objects. 'Red' is true of *a* just in case *a* is red. *But* Quine does not offer a *theory* of just what it is in which their syncategorematic character consists. He does relate it, however, to inaccessibility to quantification—indeed this seems to be almost its defining trait. My analysis, on the other hand, *explains* the syncategorematic character of predicates *without any reference to quantification.* This frees the concept of generalization from the close tie with objects and ontology which was built into classical quantification theory, and justifies the appeal to freethinking in logistics which protected our exploration of 'something'. *The role of generalization is not tied to objects,* though—trivially—that of generalization *about objects* is.

41.     Well, if predicates are simply auxiliary symbols, this entails that the connection of a statement with extra-linguistic reality does not directly involve a connection between a predicate and extra-linguistic reality. The presence of the predicate gives the names which occur in the statement a distinctive character by

virtue of which *they* are connected with extra-linguistic reality. But the names could have had a distinctive character of equal effectiveness though the statement contained no predicate.

42.    Names which have a 'larger than' between them are the linguistic counterparts of objects one of which is larger than the other. But, in the Jumblese dialect, names, one of which is placed above the other, are also the linguistic counterparts of objects one of which is larger than the other.

43.    In each case the distinctive character by virtue of which names of that character function as linguistic counterparts of objects, one of which is larger than the other, is a matter of convention. Thus instead of 'larger than' the auxiliary symbol could be 'glubber than' and, in a different Jumblese dialect, the statement made by

(6) $\begin{smallmatrix} a \\ b \end{smallmatrix}$

might be made by

(6') $\begin{smallmatrix} b \\ a \end{smallmatrix}$.

44.    Clearly a theory of linguistic representation would view the connection between either (5) or (6) and extra-linguistic reality as involving two dimensions: (a) a dimension in which each name is a linguistic counterpart of an object, and can be said to refer to that object; and (b) a dimension in which names, by virtue of having a certain character, constitute statements (in the logician's sense of 'statement' which has nothing to do with illocutionary force) and can be said to characterize the objects referred to.

45.    Thus, in the statement

(5) a is larger than b

the first name is an 'a', the second name is a 'b' and the names have the character of having a 'larger than' between them. Just *how* these facts about the names are involved in the semantical functioning of this sentence is the ultimate question with which this book is concerned. It is, however, one which must be approached with care and the right tools.

46.    Thus, as a matter of fact it will be well to retreat a bit, consolidate ground, and clear away some additional sources of misunderstanding, before advancing to the task.

47.    Let us begin by applying the above considerations to the case of one-place predicates. In this case our Tractarian principle becomes

We can *only* say that-fa by tokening an 'a' in a certain conventional style.

48.    Thus consider

(7) Red a
(8) A.

These two sentences, one in the language form of *Principia,* one in a Jumblese dialect, make the same statement. Each has as its syntactical form the character of being an 'a' written in a certain style.

49.    Notice, therefore, that (8) has two semantically relevant characters; one by virtue of which it is an 'a', a generic character which admits a wide range of determinate values; the other by virtue of which it has a certain style. This need not consist in its having a certain shape—indeed it might be a matter of size or color.[2] Thus, the fact that (8) is an 'a' is bound up with the fact that it *refers to* a, and the fact that it is an 'a' in a certain angular style is bound up with the fact that it *characterizes* a as red. Just *how* these features are bound up with reference and characterizing is, of course, the central problem of a theory of linguistic representation.

50.    We can put this by saying that 'a' is a linguistic representative or counterpart of a, and that names which are in a certain style, e.g. concatenated with a 'red', are linguistic counterparts of red objects. In the latter respect it will be useful to speak of names as having a *counterpart character*, which we can represent by the predicate 'red*'. Thus,

red* 'a's

---

[2] Wittgenstein in the *Tractatus* suggests that the compatibilities and incompatibilities of semantically significant styles might reflect the compatibilities and incompatibilities of quality spaces.

refers to 'a's which are red* as 'white dogs' refers to dogs which are white.

51.     As in the case of relational predicates, it must be stressed that *nothing in or about* (8) is doing the job done in (7) by 'red'. Obviously the fact that (8) is in a certain angular style is essential to the semantical role that it is playing. But that fact does not do the job done in (7) by 'red'. Rather it does the job which is done in (7) by the fact that 'a' is concatenated to the left with the token of the word 'red'. Thus the points made above (paragraph 39) concerning the merits and demerits of Frege's account of empirical predicates apply equally to one-place predicates.

II

52.     We have seen that from a nominalistic point of view a perspicuous dialect would represent that $x_1$ is $^2R_1$ to $x_2$ by placing tokens of '$x_1$' and '$x_2$' in a counterpart dyadic relation, $^2R_1*$, e.g. *catacorner-left to*, thus

$x_1$

$x_2$

That $x_2$ in turn is $^2R_2$ to $x_3$ might be represented by

$x_2$
$x_3$

the counterpart relation, $^2R_2*$, being *immediately above*.

53.     Notice that these representations can be combined in two ways to form a compound representation which has, in a sense, the same "content." (a) They can be combined by the logical operation of conjunction, thus:

$x_1$                    $x_2$
        and
$x_2$                    $x_3$ .

.

(b) They can be combined in one complex representation without the use of the connective 'and', thus:

$x_1$
  $x_2$
  $x_3$ .

Hence the rule of Conjunction Introduction as it applies to this case can be formulated either as

| | ${}^\backprime x_1$ | | $x_2$ | | ${}^\backprime x_1$ | | $x_2$ |
|---|---|---|---|---|---|---|---|
| from | | and | | infer | | *and* | |
| | $x_2{}^\prime$ | | $x_3{}^\prime$ | | $x_2$ | | $x_3{}^\prime$ |

or, equivalently as

| | ${}^\backprime x_1$ | | ${}^\backprime x_1$ | | $x_2$ |
|---|---|---|---|---|---|
| from | | infer | | *and* | |
| | $x_2$ | | $x_2$ | | $x_3{}^\prime$ . |
| | $x_3{}^\prime$ | | | | |

54.    It might be thought that

${}^\backprime x_1$
  $x_2$
  $x_3{}^\prime$

is only superficially different from

| ${}^\backprime x_1$ | | ${}^\backprime x_2$ |
|---|---|---|
| | and | |
| $x_2{}^\prime$ | | $x_3{}^\prime$ |

a different way of writing it, so to speak, as

'Socrates and Plato'

is equivalent by definition to

'Socrates'⌢'and'⌢'Plato'

but not

'Soc'⌢'rat'⌢'es'⌢'and'⌢'Plato'.

But this would be so only if the representation

$x_1$
$x_2$
$x_3$

were only superficially different from the sequence of representations

$x_1$     $x_2$
$x_2$,    $x_3$.

That this is *not* the case is clear from the fact that the former contains the representation

$x_1$

$x_3$

in a manner in which it is not contained in the latter.

55.     From a platonistic point of view, on the other hand, a perspicuous dialect would represent that $x_1$ and $x_2$ exemplify $^2R_1$ by placing tokens of '$x_1$' and '$x_2$' and '$^2R_1$' in a triadic relation which is the counterpart of the exemplification nexus, thus

$^2R_1[x_1,x_2]$.

That $x_2$ and $x_3$, in turn, exemplify $^2R_2$ would be represented by placing tokens of '$x_2$', '$x_3$' and '$^2R_2$' in the *same* counterpart relation, thus

$^2R_2[x_2,x_3]$.

For since the nexus or tie to be represented by the counterpart is the same in the two cases (exemplification as it pertains to dyadic relations), perspicuousness demands that the counterpart be the same.

56.     Conjunction Introduction as it applies to this case would be

from '$^2R_1[x_1,x_2]$' and '$^2R_2[x_2,x_3]$' infer '$^2R_1[x_1,x_2]$ *and* $^2R_2[x_2,x_3]$'.

57.     Notice, now, that the clothes of Jumblese could be stolen by the platonist, i.e., he could use a mode of representation which is *visually similar* to the Jumblese representation of the proposition that $x_1$ is $^2R_1$ to $x_2$, i.e.,

$x_1$

$x_2$

but, though *visually* similar, it must be differently *parsed*. To see this, one need only refer to the Tractarian axiom that

One can *only* say that objects stand in an n-adic relation, $^nR_i$, by placing the names of the objects in a counterpart n-adic relation $^nR_i*$

for this requires that the platonistic parsing of the (from its point of view) unperspicuous

$x_1$

$x_2$

and the perspicuous

$$^2R_1[x_1,x_2]$$

be brought under a common form; and this, in turn, requires that *something* in the former be functioning as the name of the (putative) *object* $^2R_1$. Since it contains no *particular* (i.e., linguistic *token*) which does the job, it must be some other (putative) constituent of the former representation which does it, i.e., *names* the *relation* $^2R_1$. The platonist finds this name in the relation *catacorner-left-to* (catacorner-left-to-ness), a *universal* rather than a particular.

58.     Thus the former is to be parsed as

the names, (1), a token of '$x_1$', (2), a token of '$x_2$', and (3), *catacorner-left-to*[3] in the triadic relation (tie) *dyadic-relational exemplification of* (3) *by* [(1),(2)].

59.     On the other hand, the latter is to be parsed as

the names, (1), a token if '$x_1$', (2), a token of '$x_2$', and (3), a token of ''$^2R_1$' in the triadic relation *linearly concatenated,* in the order (3), [(1),(2)].

60.     In each case the expression in question is construed by the platonist as a placing of the names of the objects $x_1$, $x_2$, $^2R_1$ in a conventionally selected triadic relation. The unperspicuous character of the first, or pseudo-Jumblese, representation is, for the platonist, due to the fact that in pseudo-Jumblese *universals* function directly as names, unmediated by symbol tokens.

61.     Thus, the grammatical mind's eye of the platonist "sees" the representation

$x_1$

$x_2$

not, with the nominalist, as

a token of the name '$x_1$' which is catacorner-left to a token of the name '$x_2$'

---

[3] It is, of course, essential to bear in mind that the expression 'catacorner-left-to' is being *used* and not *mentioned*. It is the relation itself, an abstract entity, which is functioning as a name.

but rather as

a token of the name '$x_1$' and a token of the name '$x_2$' which jointly exemplify the name *catacorner-left-to*.

62.    Again, whereas the nominalist sees the complex representation

$x_1$
   $x_2$
   $x_3$

as

a token of '$x_1$' catacorner-left to a token of '$x_2$' which, in turn, is above a token of '$x_3$',

the platonist "sees" it as

a token of '$x_1$' which jointly exemplifies the name *catacorner-left-to* (catacorner-left-to-ness) with a token of '$x_2$' which, in turn, jointly exemplifies the name *immediately above* (immediate-above-ness) with a token of '$x_3$'.

63.    Compare the latter with the platonist's parsing of what for him is a perspicuous text

$$^2R_1[x_1,x_2].\ ^2R_2[x_2,x_3].^4$$

The parsing is

(1), a token of '$x_1$', (2), a token of '$x_2$', (3), a token of '$^2R_1$', linearly con-

---

[4] *Nota Bene:* This expression is not a *conjunction* but rather a *sequence* of two sentence tokens, each of which is punctuated with a full stop or period. To see it as thus punctuated is equivalent to seeing it *as* a sequence or two *sentences*. In this sense, the punctuation is superfluous, given that the language has tidy formation rules.

catenated in the order (3), [(1),(2)]; followed by (4), a token of 'x$_2$', (5), a token of 'x$_3$', (6), a token of '$^2$R$_2$', linearly concatenated in the order (6), [(4),(5)].

64.     Notice that whereas Jumblese and pseudo-Jumblese have two ways of saying what is said by the conjunctive proposition,

$$x_1 \qquad\qquad x_2$$
$$\text{and}$$
$$x_2 \qquad\qquad x_3$$

namely,

$$x_1 \qquad\qquad x_2$$
$$. \qquad\qquad .$$
$$x_2 \qquad\qquad x_3$$

where the dots are full stops, and

$$x_1$$
$$x_2$$
$$x_3$$

perspicuous platonese has only one, i.e.,

$$^2R_1[x_1,x_2].\ ^2R_2[x_2,x_3]..$$

65.     This fact is highly relevant to the central role, in an adequate nominalistic theory of linguistic representation, of a stratum of complex representations (maps), the constituents of which have an *empirical* structure. As having this empirical form (i.e., as sign design tokens) they function in the uniformities of rule-governed linguistic behavior.

66.     The formation rules of the language pick out items having certain *empirical*

forms to have *logical* form in the sense of *predicational* form,[5] i.e. they function as atomic sentences, but do not, *as functioning in this stratum*, have logical form in the sense of *undergoing* logical operations (truth-functional combination, quantification), although, as constituents of a *representational system*, they are *subject to* these operations either directly (by wearing, so to speak, another hat) or *indirectly* by being correlated with (translatable into) other designs which are directly subject to these operations.

67.    In the concluding chapter, I shall be exploring the role of mapping in (an adequate) nominalistic theory of representation. My present purpose has been to make clear that in a *platonistic* ontology, atomic *sentences* map objects, by virtue of (a) a *naming* relationship and (b) a principle of mapping according to which

*Concatenations* of names map *exemplifications of* universals by particulars

and according to which, therefore, the *multiplicity* of the varieties of mapping is simply the *multiplicity* of modes of exemplification, i.e., monadic, dyadic, triadic, etc. (if more are needed).

68.    For the perceptive nominalist, on the other hand, the varieties of mapping are as multiple as simple *matter-of-factual* qualities and relations.[6]

### III

69.    At the beginning of this chapter, I pointed out that it is "obvious that the words 'red' and 'green' contribute *something* to the meaning" of the sentences 'a is red' and 'a is green', and that "it is equally obvious that there must be *something* in the extra-linguistic domain which corresponds to this contribution and helps account for the fact that the first of these statements is true, the second false." I proceeded to warn against assuming that the *something* in question is either an *object* or a Fregean non-object. What *is* the something? It may seem anti-climactic

---

[5] This is not to say that an item could have predicational form by virtue of the formation rules alone. There could not be a representational system which had "formation rules" only. The point of these remarks is to distinguish different senses of 'logical form'.

[6] It should be obvious that the ultimate rationale of an absolute distinction between "simple" and "complex" characteristics (predicative expressions) requires a reference to the laws (true law-like statements) in which these characteristics (predicative expressions) are involved. But to unpack *this* it would be necessary to explore the concept of an *ideal* representation of *our* world.

to say

> red objects and green objects

yet this is, if not the end, at least the beginning of the end of a sound theory of linguistic representation. For, to use an Irish bull (in fact, the material mode of speech) *red objects* is neither an object nor a *Fregean non-object*. That is, on the formal mode, 'red objects' is neither a singular term nor a *Fregean* predicate.

70.     I have italicized 'Fregean' because of the specifics of Frege's theory. There is, however, a sense in which the views I have been developing in this chapter are very much in the spirit of Frege's *intuitions*. 'Red objects' may be neither a name nor a Fregean predicate, but is it not a virtual class abstract and hence, after all, a predicate? Furthermore, given our reconstruction (in chapter 2, paragraphs 62-4) of

> 'Man' refers to man

in terms of

> 'Man' refers to men

can we not say that *men* are the *something* in the extra-linguistic domain which contributes to the explanation of why 'Tom is a man' is true?

71.     The "real relation" which underlies the fact that 'man' refers to men must surely be a real relation between the word 'man' and men, a relation to be formulated in terms of generalizations having subjunctive form, which specify uniformities in which expression-tokens (including sentences containing the word 'man') and extra-linguistic objects (including men) are involved. What these uniformities might be, and how they are to be classified, are questions to which I shall return.

72.     The point with which I shall conclude this chapter is that the generalizations in question do not, so to speak, *separately* relate 'red' to red things nor 'man' to men. They relate *sentential* expressions containing 'red' to red things and *sentential* expressions containing 'man' to men. For, after all, if our account of predication is correct, the kind of connection involved must also apply to the

Jumblese dialect, *in which there are no predicative expressions.*

73.    Thus in looking for the matter-of-factual foundation of reference, we must avoid that picture according to which the connection between 'a is red' and the non-linguistic domain is a composition function of a connection between 'a' and a and a connection of 'red' with red objects. For it is this picture which generates the perennial temptation to assimilate the semantical function of 'red' to that of 'a', and hence to think of 'red' as referring *either* to an object (redness) *or* a non-object *( ) is red.* The result in either case is a metaphysics which construes red things as particulars which, in the one case, are tied by 'exemplify' to the attribute redness and which, in the other, "saturate" the gappy (predicative) entity, *( ) is red.*

74.    We must, instead, take even more seriously than Frege succeeded in doing the *primacy of the sentential* role. A correct theory of predication, which, paradoxically, stresses the dispensability of predicates, enables us to understand how 'red' refers to red things without deriving this fact from a more basic relation between 'red', or even sentences of the form 'x is red', and an unsaturated (or predicative) entity, *( ) is red.*

75.    A Fregean might attempt to mitigate the disagreement by arguing that on my own account 'x is red' is logically equivalent to 'x is a red thing', and, hence, 'x and y are red' to 'x and y are red things'. The difference between 'x is red' and 'x is a red thing', and between 'red thing' and 'red things' is, he continues, superficial. He, therefore, denies that in any interesting sense he *derives* the relation between sentences of the form 'x is red' and red things from a more basic relation between 'x is red' and an unsaturated (or predicative) entity, *( ) is red, as contrasted with* the unsaturated (or predicative) entity, *( ) is(are) (a) red thing(s).* But all this shows is how close Frege's theory comes to incorporating a correct theory of predication and to enabling a correct theory of the referential role of predicates.

76.    For the crucial point remains that the unsaturated (or predicative) entity, *( ) is(are) (a) red thing(s),* is not the same as *red things.* The word 'predicative' gives the show away, for, pace Wittgenstein, the extra-linguistic domain consists of *objects, not facts.* To put it bluntly, propositional form belongs only in the linguistic and conceptual orders. Red things do *not* have propositional form, and it is, therefore, not an "unsaturated" (or predicative) entity— whether *( ) is red* or *( ) is(are) (a) red thing(s),* both amply endowed with predicative form—which is the extra-linguistic term of the matter-of-factual relation involved in the

referential role of 'red'.

77. These remarks, however, do little more than indicate the dimensions of the task which remains in constructing a theory of linguistic representation. But before they can be elaborated, it is necessary to supplement them by a theory of meaning which takes account, in Fregean terms, of sense as well as reference.

## 4  MEANING AND ONTOLOGY*

I

1.      Gilbert Harman, in his admirable paper "Three Levels of Meaning,"[1] distinguishes three approaches which philosophers have taken in attempting to clarify what it is for linguistic expressions to have meaning. Each of these approaches finds the Ariadne thread which is to guide us through the labyrinth of semantics in a different function of language. One group takes as its central theme the idea that language is, so to speak, the very medium in which we think, at least at the distinctively human level. Another finds its clue in the fact of communication. A third focuses its attention on the kinship between such linguistic acts as stating and promising and a broad spectrum of social practices.

2.      Harman, correctly, in my opinion, points out that viewed as three attempts to answer one and the same question, these strategies involve serious confusions, and that those who take them to be such have inevitably become entangled in fruitless controversies. He also, somewhat generously I think, recommends that we view them as attempts to answer three different questions and suggests, accordingly, that we refrain from criticizing any one of them "for failing to do what can be done only by a theory of meaning of another level."[2]

3.      Harman calls approaches to meaning of these three types "theories of meaning of level 1, 2 and 3, respectively." He correctly, I think, considers the approach to meaning which construes language as the medium in which we think

---

*This chapter is in large part a revised version of "Meaning as Functional Classification" (MFC) which appeared in J.C. Troyer and S.C. Wheeler, III (eds.) *Intentionality, Language and Translation*, Dordrecht-Holland, 1974.

[1] *The Journal of Philosophy* 65 (1968), 590-602. This paper was reprinted in *Semantics* (ed. by D.D. Steinberg and L.A. Jakobovits), Cambridge, England, 1971. Page references will be to the latter.

[2] *Ibid.*, p. 71.

to be fundamental, and, accordingly, of "level 1." He points out that a theory of level 2, i.e., a theory of communication (of thoughts), presupposes a theory of level 1 that would say what various thoughts are. Similarly, a theory of level 3 (i.e., an account of linguistic acts) must almost always presuppose a theory of level 2 (since in making a statement, for example, as in promising, one must communicate the relevant information). He concludes that "a theory of one level does not provide a good theory of another level. A theory of the meaning of thoughts does not provide a good account of communication. A theory of meaning and communication does not provide a good account of speech acts."[3]

4.      Now one need not agree that even distinctively human thinking is literally done 'in words', in order to appreciate the importance of Harman's three-tiered approach to theories of meaning. For even if, as I do, one finds a reference to "inner conceptual episodes" which are only in an analogical sense "verbal" to be an indispensable feature of what might be called fine-grained psychological explanations, it is nevertheless possible to construe this "fine-grained" framework as a theoretical enrichment of a "coarse grained" explanatory framework which simply *equates* thinking with processes which are "verbal"—if I may so put it—in the literal sense, i.e., are sequences of verbal behavior and propensities pertaining thereto.

5.      To make a serious contribution to a non-cartesian philosophy of mind, this "coarse grained" framework must be construed as methodologically autonomous in the sense that it contains categories of sense and reference, meaning and truth which can be fully explicated without any reference to non-verbal "inner conceptual episodes." Thus envisaged, this behavioristic stratum of psychological explanation could characterize linguistic episodes *directly* in semantical terms, i.e., without overt or covert reference to the "inner conceptual episodes" which, from the standpoint of the enriched framework, are involved in the "finer grained" explanation of their occurrence.

6.      Just as micro-physical theories have typically made use of conceptually independent models at the perceptual level, so, I shall argue in the next chapter, the explanatory function of "inner conceptual episodes" can be construed as resting upon an autonomous proto-psychological framework in which linguistic activity is described, explained and evaluated without reference to the framework of

[3] *Ibid.*, p. 68.

"mental acts" which it supports.

7.      On the assumption that such a proto-psychological framework can be isolated, I shall present it in the guise of a claim that thinking at the characteristically human level simply *is* what is described by this framework. I shall refer to this claim as Verbal Behaviorism (VB). I do not, of course, offer it as an adequate account of thinking; it is, indeed, radically oversimplified. I believe, however, that it provides a useful strategy for clarifying certain key issues in the philosophy of language.

8.      With these qualifications, then, the enterprise on which I am embarking can be characterized as the construction of a "level 1 theory of meaning" in Harman's sense of the phrase.

## II

9.      According to VB, then, thinking 'that-p', where this means 'having the thought occur to one that-p' has its *primary* sense *saying* 'p', and a *secondary* sense in which it stands for a short term proximate propensity to say 'p'. Propensities tend to be actualized (a logical point about the term); when they are not, we speak of them as, for example, "blocked". The VB I am constructing sees the relevant inhibiting factor which blocks a saying that-p as that of not being in a thinking-out-loud frame of mind. If one were theorizing about it, one might use the model of a general "on-off" switch which gets into the child's "wiring diagram" when he learns to keep his thoughts to himself.

10.     Again, a thinking-out-loud that-fa is to be construed as a candid utterance (by one who speaks a regimented PMese language) of 'fa' which realizes a fragment of the conceptual functions of 'f' and 'a' and is related to their other conceptual functions, as a placing of a pawn on a chess board in the course of a game *realizes* a fragment of the function of a pawn and is related to its other chess functions.

11.     Notice that I have been treating that-clauses as quoted expressions, thus, in the above account

        the thought that 2 + 2 = 4 occurred to Jones

becomes

Jones said (or had a short term proximate propensity to say) '2 + 2 = 4'.

For, as VB sees it, if thinking is verbal activity, then ascribing a certain thought to a person by the use of "indirect discourse" is not simply analogous to, but identical with, saying what someone has said (or was disposed to say).

12.  The above equation of quoting with indirect discourse is, of course, not only *parochial*, in that it views the latter in the context of only one language—the speaker's—it also fails to take into account the fact that even with respect to one and the same language people can make non-trivially different utterances 'p', 'q', 'r' and nevertheless be correctly described as saying that-p. The clarification of this fact requires an account of similarity of meaning and its relation to indirect discourse.

13.  In any ordinary sense, of course, saying 'p' is an action or performance. From the point of view of this paper, to characterize an utterance as a "saying," as the verb 'to say' is ordinarily used, permits it to be either a spontaneous thinking-out-loud that-p or a deliberate use of words to achieve a purpose. Here, on the other hand, the verb 'to say' is being used in a *contrived* sense in which these options are closed, and the utterance specifically construed as a spontaneous or candid thinking-out-loud.

14.  Mental acts in the Cartesian or Aristotelian sense are, of course, not *actions*, but rather *actualities*, and consequently the thinkings-out-loud which I am offering as a model for classical mental acts construed as elements in a finer grained explanatory framework must not be thought of as linguistic actions.

15.  On the other hand, even if an individual mental *act*, thus the act of thinking that-fa, is not itself an *action*, it may well occur in a sequence of mental acts which *as sequence* constitutes a mental action, e.g., the action of pondering whether or not to undertake a certain line of conduct. Correspondingly, an act of thinking-out-loud that-fa may well occur in a sequence of thinking-out-louds which constitutes the *action* of pondering-out-loud whether or not to engage in that line of conduct, even though the pondering-out-loud is not an *other*-directed or *social* action.[4] Thus the Verbal Behaviorist can construe actions of pondering-out-loud as the model for the finer grained conception of what it is to ponder *in*

---

[4] The topic of linguistic behavior in the context of communication will be explored in the next chapter.

*foro interno.*

16.     If all full-fledged linguistic episodes were actions, then learning a language would be learning a repertoire of actions. This way of looking at language gives comfort to Cartesians in the following way. Obviously not all thoughts are actions. Indeed such central kinds of thought as perceptual takings, inferences, and volitions are not actions for the simple reason that they are not the sort of thing which can be done intentionally or that one can decide to do. One can decide *to look* in the next room, but not *to take there to be a burglar* in the next room. Of course there *are* mental actions, thus, working on a mathematical problem or pondering what to wear. But as pointed out above, they consist of chains of thoughts which are not themselves actions.

17.     If all *linguistic* episodes were actions, then all conceptually meaningful non-actions would have to be non-linguistic and, hence, thoughts in something like the Cartesian sense. It would be at this *non-linguistic* level that the thinking would occur by virtue of which *linguistic* activity could realize intentions and constitute a domain of actions. It is but a step from this to construing language as essentially an instrument for "expressing thoughts"—when one is being candid—and, in general, for leading others to believe that one believes that-p (or intends that-p), and perhaps intends that they believe that one intends that they so believe, etc. All linguistic episodes would be actions; not just those which are statings, promisings, warnings, etc.

### III

18.     One can imagine a child to learn a rudimentary language in terms of which he can perceive, draw inferences, and act. In doing so, he begins by uttering noises which *sound like* words and sentences and ends by uttering noises which are words and sentences. We might use quoted words to describe what he is doing at both stages, but in the earlier stage we are classifying his utterances as *sounds* and only by courtesy and anticipation as *words*. Only when the child has got the hang of how his utterances function in the language can he be properly characterized as saying 'This is a book' or 'It is not raining' or 'Lightning, so shortly thunder'.

19.     I offer the following as an initial or working description of the thesis I wish to defend. To say *what* a person says, or, more generally, to say *what* a kind of utterance says, is to give a functional classification of the utterance. This

functional classification involves a special (illustrating) use of expressions with which the addressee is presumed to be familiar, i.e., which are, so to speak, in his background language.

20. Some of the functions with respect to which utterances are classified are purely intralinguistic (syntactical) and, in simple cases, are correlated with formation and transformation rules as described in classical logical syntax. Others concern language as a response to sensory stimulation by environmental objects— thus, candidly saying, or having the short term propensity to say, 'Here is a penny', or 'This table is red'. Still others concern the connection of practical thinking with behavior.

21. All these dimensions of functioning recur at the meta-linguistic level in the language in which we respond to verbal behavior, draw inferences about verbal behavior and engage in practical thinking about verbal behavior—i.e., practical thinking-out-loud (or propensities to think-out-loud) about thinking-out-loud (or propensities to think-out-loud).

22. Thus when we characterize a person's utterances by using a quoted expression, we imply that the utterance is an instance of certain specific ways of functioning. For example, it would be absurd to say

> Tom *said* (as contrasted with "uttered the noises") 'It is *not* raining', but, even in serious frames of mind and in contexts in which the state of the weather is of great practical importance, can be disposed to think-out-loud 'It is raining *and* it is *not* raining'.

Thus, to characterize a person's utterance by the use of quoted sentences containing logical words is to imply that the corresponding sounds function properly in the verbal behavior in question; and hence to imply that the uniformities characteristic of these ways of functioning are present in his thinkings-out-loud and proximate propensities to think-out-loud.

23. It should be stressed that the uniformities involved in meaningful verbal behavior include *negative* uniformities, i.e., the avoidance of certain combinations, as well as *positive* uniformities, i.e., uniformities of concomitance. Indeed, negative uniformities play by far the more important role, and the rules which govern them are to be construed as *constraints* rather than incentives.

24. The functioning which gives the utterances of one who has learned a lan-

guage their meaning *can* exist merely at the level of uniformities as in the case of the fledgling speaker. Those who train him, thus his parents, think about these functionings and attempt to ensure that his verbal behavior exemplifies them. In this respect, the trainer operates not only at the level of the trainee, thinking thoughts about things, but also at that higher level which is thinking thoughts about the functions by virtue of which first level language has the meanings it does. In traditional terms, the trainer knows the *rules* which govern the *correct* functioning of the language. The language learner begins by *conforming* to these rules without grasping them himself.

25.     Only subsequently does the language learner become a full-fledged member of the linguistic community, who thinks thoughts (theoretical and practical) not only about *non-linguistic* items, but also about *linguistic* items, i.e., from the point of view of VB, about *first level* thoughts.

26.     He has then developed from being the object of training and criticism by others to the stage at which he can train and criticize other language users and even himself. Indeed he has now reached the level at which he can formulate new and sophisticated standards in terms of which to reshape his language and develop new modes of thought.

27.     The key to the concept of a linguistic rule is its complex relation to pattern-governed linguistic behavior. The general concept of pattern-governed behavior is a familiar one. Roughly it is the concept of behavior which exhibits a pattern, not because it is brought about by the intention that it exhibit this pattern, but because the propensity to emit behavior of the pattern has been selectively reinforced, and the propensity to emit behavior which does not conform to this pattern selectively extinguished. A useful analogy is the natural selection which results in the patterns of behavior which constitutes the so-called language of bees.[5]

28.     If pattern-governed behavior can arise by "natural" selection, it can also arise by purposive selection on the part of trainers. They can be construed as reasoning:

> Patterned behavior of such and such a kind *ought to be* exhibited by trainees; hence we, the trainers, *ought to do* this and that, as likely to bring it about that

---

[5] See "Some Reflections on Language Games" SRLG(24), reprinted as Chapter II in SPR.

it *is* exhibited.

29.    The basic point to bear in mind is that

a piece of pattern-governed behavior is *as such* not an action (though actions can consist of sequences of pattern-governed behavior)

and

is correct or incorrect, not as *actions* are correct or incorrect, but as events which are not actions are correct or incorrect.

An obvious example of the latter would be the correctness of *feeling sorrow* for someone who is bereaved.

30.    'This is red', as a pattern-governed response to red objects, is not an action. Yet it is covered by a rule and, indeed, a rule which is involved in the explanation of its occurrence. The rule which directly covers it is, however, an ought-to-be, and it is involved in the explanation by virtue of the fact that it was envisaged by the trainers who assisted the speaker in acquiring his linguistic ability. Trainees conform to *ought-to-bes* because trainers obey corresponding *ought-to-dos*.

IV

31.    Essential to any language are three types of pattern-governed linguistic behavior.

(1)    Language Entry Transitions: The speaker responds, *ceteris paribus*, to objects in perceptual situations, and to certain states of himself, with appropriate linguistic activity.

(2)    Intralinguistic Transitions:[6] The speaker's linguistic conceptual episodes tend to occur in patterns of valid inference (theoretical and practical) and tend not to occur in patterns which violate logical

---

[6] In the paper referred to in the previous footnote I used 'moves' instead of 'transitions', but the former is so clearly an action word that its use in this context must inevitably reinforce the tendency to think of languagings as actions, warned against in paragraph 16 above.

principles.[7]

(3)     Language Departure Transitions: The speaker responds, *ceteris paribus*, to such linguistic conceptual episodes as 'I will now raise my hand' with an upward motion of the hand, etc.

32.     It is essential to note that not only are the abilities to engage in such thinkings-out-loud *acquired* as pattern-governed activity, they *remain* pattern-governed activity. The linguistic activities which are perceptual takings, inferences and volitions *never* become *obeyings* of *ought to do* rules. Thus, compare

(A)    Jones    All men are mortal.
                      So, no non-mortals are men.

(B)    Smith    If I am entitled to 'All men are mortal', I am entitled to 'No non-mortals are men'.
                      I am entitled to the former, I state it thus:
                            All men are mortal.
                      So, I am entitled to the latter, I state it thus:
                            No non-mortals are men.

In each case the upshot contains the sequence: 'All men are mortal', 'No non-mortals are men'. But only Jones is *inferring* the latter from the former. Smith exhibits a piece of practical reasoning about linguistic entitlements which he proceeds to exercise.

33.     It must also be stressed that the concept of pattern should not be interpreted narrowly. Thus, one must include among ones paradigms not only acquiring a propensity to exhibit uniformities of the kind illustrated by the pattern

All --- is ...
This is ---
So, this is ...

but also propensities of the kind which Wittgenstein describes as "knowing how

---

[7]Note the stress on negative uniformities in paragraph 23 above.

to go on." There are many dimensions of knowing how to go on, and the recursive patterns stressed by structural linguistics are essential to the workings of language. They can, however, and, indeed, must be included in an adequate conception of pattern-governed behavior. Pattern-governed behavior may involve a routine, but it need not be routine.

34.    It is the pattern-governed activities of perception, inference and volition, themselves essentially non-actions, which underlie and make possible the domain of actions, linguistic and nonlinguistic. Thus the trainee acquires not only the repertoire of pattern-governed linguistic behavior which is language about non-linguistic items, but also that extended repertoire which is language about linguistic as well as non-linguistic items. He is able to classify items in linguistic kinds and to engage in theoretical and practical reasoning about his linguistic behavior. Language entry transitions now include 'This is a '2 + 2 = 4'' as well as 'This is a table'. Language departure transitions include, 'I will say '2 + 2= 4'' followed by a saying of '2 + 2 = 4', as well as 'I will raise my hand' followed by a raising of the hand.[8] The trainee acquires the ability to language about languagings, to criticize languagings, including his own; he can become one who trains himself.

35.    It would be a mistake to suppose that a language is learned as a layer cake is constructed: *first* the object language, *then* a meta-language, then a meta-meta-language, etc.,[9] or, *first*, descriptive expressions, *then* logical words, *then* expressions of intention, etc. The language learner gropes in all these dimensions simultaneously. And each level of achievement is more accurately pictured as a falling of things belonging to different dimensions into place, rather than addition of a new story to a building.

V

36.    Notice that according to the VB conception of thinking, we can distinguish

---

[8] *A raising* of the hand can be construed, roughly, as a rising of the hand *qua* something which can be brought about by a volition to have one's hand rise. By absorption, the latter becomes a volition to *raise* one's hand. According to the Verbal Behaviorist, of course, a volition is a thinking-out-loud or a proximate propensity to think-out-loud, 'I will...'. For a more detailed account of the VB conception of practical thinking, see my paper "Actions and Events" AAE(78).

[9] It is perhaps worth noting that the concept of pattern-governed linguistic behavior must be extended to include the recursive know-how involved in "going up the meta-language hierarchy."

clearly between the *functional* role of utterances and the *phomenic* description of the linguistic materials which embody or are the "vehicles" of these functions. It is a most significant fact that the classical conception of thought as "inner speech" (Mentalese) draws no such clear distinction between the conceptual functions of Mentalese symbols and the materials which serve as the *vehicle* of these functions. Yet, if the analogy between thinking, classically construed, and overt linguistic behavior is to be a reasonably positive one, the idea that there must be inner-linguistic *vehicles* (materials) would seem to be a reasonable one. It is often thought that imagery is the vehicle of Mentalese—but there doesn't seem to be enough imagery to go around. And, indeed, the idea of imageless thought is by no means incoherent. What might the vehicle be?

37.     From the point of view of this chapter, the classical conception of thoughts as pure occurrents is motivated by the familiar attempt to relate changes in *dispositional properties* to changes in *underlying non-dispositional* states. The emptiness of the classical account of thought episodes can be explained by the fact that it uses as its model for the description of the *intrinsic* nature of mental acts (i.e. what they "consist of") aspects of linguistic activity which are largely functional in character.[10] Thus, by and large, it is the *non-functional* aspects of the linguistic model which are, save in their most generic aspects, disregarded. After all, leaving aside functional considerations, thoughts *are* neuro-physiological processes; and this is an idea which no arm-chair philosophizing could turn into cash.

## VI

38.     How does 'that-fa' function in 'Jones says that-fa'[11] (where 'says' is used in the sense of 'thinks-out-loud')? To answer this question, we must ask a prior question:

---

[10] See "Metaphysics and the Concept of the Person" MP(68), reprinted in KTM.

[11] The fact that in this chapter the problem of meaning is discussed with reference to subject-predicate languages should not lead the reader to forget the fundamental considerations pertaining to the role of predicates advanced in the preceding chapter. The argument of the present chapter will be found to reinforce the thesis that the semantical role of 'red', for example, does not include a relation to an extra-linguistic entity, redness or *( ) is red* [cf. red things].

How does ' 'fa' ' function in 'Jones says 'fa' '?

The answer is that ' 'fa' ' functions as an adverbial modifier of the verb 'says'. Language can be written, spoken, gesticulated, etc., and 'says' serves to pin down the modality of a languaging to *utterance*. If speech were the only modality, or if we abstract from a difference of modality, we could replace

> Jones says 'fa'

by

> Jones 'fa's,

i.e., use the expression-cum-quotes as a verb. Roughly, to 'fa' would be first to 'f' and then to 'a'.

39.　It is because there is a range of verbal activities involving the uttering of 'fa', e.g., asserting, repeating, etc., that we give it the status of an adverb and hence, in effect, require that even in the case of sheer thinking-out-loud there be a verb which it modifies. This is one source of the illusion that the concept of uttering '$2 + 2 = 4$' *assertively* (where the latter does not connote the illocutionary act of asserting) requires the neustic-phrastic distinction.

40.　Although our immediate model for mental acts is thinking-out-loud and consists, therefore, of linguistic activities of persons, rather than of such linguistic objects produced by persons as inscriptions or recordings, it will enable us to by-pass central issues in the ontology of substances, acts (events, states) and manners (adverbial entities) if we use as our primary linguistic objects the direct by-products of thinking-in-writing, i.e., inscriptions.

41.　What is it, then, to characterize an inscription as an 'fa'? Clearly, it is to characterize it as a linear concatenation of an of an 'f' with an 'a'. Thus the following inscription

> fa

is an 'f' concatenated to the right with an 'a'. Representing this mode of concatenation by '⌢', the above inscription is an 'f⌢'a'. Thus an 'fa' = an 'f⌢'a'[12] = an 'f⌢an 'a'[13].

42.    The expressions

'f', 'a', 'fa', 'f⌢'a',

are sortal predicates which classify linguistic tokens. The classification is partly *descriptive*, thus in terms of shape (or sound) and arrangement. It is also and, for our purposes, more importantly *functional*. Above all, the sortal predicates are "illustrating." Thus

t is an 'f'

tells us that t, belonging to a certain language L, is of a *descriptive* character falling within a certain range of which the design of the item within the single quotes is a representative sample,[14] and also tells us that (if t is in a primary sense an 'f', i.e., is produced by a thinking-in-writing) it is functioning as do items having such designs in language L.

43.    Now it is clearly possible to envisage illustrating sortals which apply to items in any language which (*vis à vis* other expressions in the language to which they belong) function as do the illustrated items in a certain base language, the ability to use which is presupposed. This language, for purposes of philosophical reconstruction, can be equated with *our* language *here* and *now*.

44.    As far as descriptive criteria are concerned, such sortals would require only those most generic features which must be present, in some determinate form or other, in order for expressions to perform the relevant functions. Thus,

(1) 'Oder's (in G) are •or•s

would say of 'oder's that they function along with other expressions in German as do •or•s. The criteria which an item must satisfy to be an •or• are a matter of its

---

[12] Cf. 'a(cat on a mat)', which has the form 'aK'.

[13] Cf. 'a (cat) on a (mat)' which has the form 'a K₁ on a K₂'.

[14] I.e., as Davidson points out, an essential part of the "sense" of the single quotes is to say 'this item'.

functioning, in respects deemed relevant[15] as do 'or's in the illustrating language, in the present case a professional dialect of English.

45.     Again

(2) '*Sokrates*'s (in German) are •Socrates•s

would say of proper tokens of the name '*Sokrates*' in German that they are •Socrates•s, where the criterion for being a •Socrates• is to function in thinking-out-loud contexts as do 'Socrates's in the illustrating language to which the quoting device is applied. Obviously the sense of 'name' relevant to this context is not that of 'name candidate', i.e., the sense in which '*Sokrates*' might be found in a list of eligible names for race horses.

46.     One is tempted to say that the function in question is that of being used to refer to a certain Greek philosopher. But it is a mistake to tie the semantical concept of reference too closely to referring as an illocutionary act.

47.     It would seem a natural extension of the above to apply the above strategy first to predicates

(3) '*rot*'s (in G) are •red•s

and then to propositional expressions

(4) '*a ist rot*'s (in G) are •a is red•s.

Omitting the copula, as more essential to tense indication than predication, and turning to schematic forms, we might commit ourselves to the idea that

---

[15] Note that the criteria for these sortals are flexible and context dependent. What counts as an •or• in one classificatory context may be classified as *like* an •or• in another. If Germans were to use '*oder*' only in the inclusive sense and we were to use 'or' only in the exclusive sense, we might, nevertheless, for some purposes, classify '*oder*'s as •or•s, taking as our criteria what the two functions of 'or' as it is *actually* used have in common. In this case '•or•' would be a generic functional classification, and we would distinguish its inclusive and exclusive species, though the only species for which we had an illustrating classification would be the latter. In other contexts the criteria for being an •or• might be more specific, thus to function *exactly* as do the exclusive 'or's of the background language. In this case '*oder*'s would not be •or•s, though they would, of course, be functionally *similar*.

(5) t is an •fa•

tells us, by the use of the illustrating functional classification, '•fa•', that token t
is functioning in some language as would an 'f' concatenated with an 'a' in our
language.

48.     The above remarks have been based on the idea of an illustrating-functional
classification of linguistic objects (inscriptions and the like) which are the *prod-
ucts* of—as I put it—thinking-in-writing. Before pressing the strategy, it is time
to pay a fleeting respect to the fact that the primary mode of being of the linguistic
is in the linguistic activity of persons.

49.     Now

(1) Jones said '2 + 2 = 4'

is obviously not to be identified with

(2) Jones uttered '2 + 2 = 4'

where this simply tells us that Jones produced sounds of a kind conventionally
associated with the shape of which *those* (the ones between the quotes) are
samples.

50.     What is the difference? The answer clearly has *something* to do with
"meaning." We are tempted to say that

(1) = Jones uttered '2 + 2 = 4' *as meaning* 2 + 2 = 4.

This is not incorrect but also not illuminating.

51.     Thus consider the following objection to VB:

Surely, it will be said, thinking that-p isn't just saying that-p—even candidly
saying that-p as you have characterized it. For thinking-out-loud that-p involves
*knowing the meaning* of what one says, and surely this is no mere matter of
producing sound!

52.     To this the obvious answer is that while there is all the difference in the

world between parroting words and thinking-out-loud in words, the difference does not consist in the latter involving a non-linguistic "knowing the meaning" of what one utters. Rather the utterances one makes in thinking-out-loud cohere with one another and with the context in which they occur in a way which is absent in mere parroting.

53.     Furthermore, the relevant sense of "knowing the meaning of words" (which is a form of what Ryle has called *knowing how*) must be carefully distinguished from knowing the meaning of words in the sense of being able to talk about them as a lexicographer might—thus, in defining them.

54.     Mastery of the language involves the latter as well as the former ability. Indeed they are *both* forms of *know how*, but at different levels—one at the "object language" level, the other at the "meta-language" level.

55.     To put our finger on what is involved, it will be useful once again to turn our attention away from language as *activity* to language as *product*, thus inscriptions, recordings and the like. If we can understand the meaning of 'meaning' in the context, say, of inscriptions, we shall not be far from understanding what it is to speak of the meaning of verbal activity, and, ultimately, the intentionality of inner conceptual episodes.

## VII

56.     To come, at last, to grips with the central topic of this chapter, consider the old chestnut

(3) '*Und*' (in German) means *and*.

Two things are to be noted: (a) The subject of this sentence is a singular term. (b) The word with which it ends is an unusual use of the word 'and', for it is not serving as a sentential connective. Let me take up these two points in order.

57.     Many philosophers have succumbed to the temptation to construe the subject of (3) as the name of a linguistic abstract entity, the German word 'und' as a universal which can (and does) have many instances. Yet this is a mistake which can (and does) cause irreparable damage. There are, indeed, many 'und's, and they are, indeed, *instances* of a certain kind—'*und*'-kind, we may call it. There are also many lions and they are instances of lion-kind.

58.    But it is important to distinguish between two singular terms which are in the neighborhood of the sortal predicate 'lion'. There is, in the first place, the singular term which belongs in the context

... is a non-empty class.

Ordinary language has no neat expression which does this job. The phrase 'the class of lions' will do.

59.    But there are also such terms as 'the lion' or 'a lion' or 'any lion', as in

The lion (or a lion, or any lion) is tawny

where these are *roughly* equivalent in meaning to

All lions are tawny.

Consider, also, 'man' as in

Man is a featherless biped.[16]

I call such singular terms 'distributive terms' (DSTs)[17].

60.    Notice that although there are monster lions, e.g., malformed lions with five legs, this fact does not impugn the truth of

The lion is a quadruped.

Normal lions have four legs. Similarly, the design *und* as it occurs in correctly

---

[16] This use of 'man' must be carefully distinguished from 'man' as in 'Man is a species', where it is a meta-linguistic sortal in the sense which will shortly be defined.

[17] See my "Abstract Entities" AE(48), reprinted as chapter III in my PPME. Notice that I am *not* saying that all expressions of the form 'the K' which are not definite descriptions of an individual K are DSTs. Thus in 'The lion once roamed the western plains', the subject is not a DST, for, though its sense is roughly equivalent to 'Lions once roamed the western plains', it is not even remotely equivalent to 'All lions once roamed the western plains'.

patterned (grammatical) German texts is an 'und'.[18]

61.     Thus the correct interpretation of the subject of (3) treats it not as an abstract singular term which designates an abstract entity, but as a distributive singular term. In other words (3) is, for our purposes, identical in sense with

(3$^1$) The (or an, or any) '*und*' (in German) means *and*

*or equivalently, with*

(3$^2$) '*Und*'s (in German) mean *and*.

62.     The second point to be noted about (3) was that it involved an atypical use of the word 'and', for it is clearly not functioning as a sentential connective. A natural move is to construe the context as a quoting one. This idea may tempt one to rewrite (3) as

(3$^3$) '*und*' (in German) means 'and'.

But quoting contexts are often such that to leave them unchanged while adding quotes to the quoted item changes the sense. And it is clear that (3) doesn't merely tell us that 'und' and 'and' *have the same meaning*; it in some sense *gives* the meaning.

63.     I have argued that the correct analysis of (3) is

(3$^4$) '*Und*'s (in German) are •and•s

where to be an •and• is to be an item in any language which functions as 'and' does in our language. Roughly, to say what an expression means is to classify it func-

---

[18] Of course, in an *extended* sense an *und*-shaped heap of sand blowing in the wind can be said to be a token of the word '*und*'—and the pages finally typed by the famous industrious monkeys, a copy of Shakespeare's plays.

tionally by means of an illustrating sortal.[19]

64.     According to this analysis, *meaning is not a relation* for the very simple reason that 'means' is a *specialized form of the copula*.[20] Again, the meaning of an expression is its "use" (in the sense of function) in that to say what an expression means is to classify it by means of an illustrating functional sortal.

65.     Notice that instead of "giving" the complex function of '*und*' (in German) by using an illustrating functional sortal, we could, instead, have formulated the grammatical rules and, in particular, the rules of logical syntax which govern the word '*und*' in the German language. The rule-governed uniformities (not all of which, of course, are purely syntactical) which constitute a language (including our own) can, *in principle,* be exhaustively described without the use of meaning statements, including those to be discussed below. In practice, however, the use of meaning statements (translation) is indispensable, for it provides a way of mobilizing our linguistic intuitions to classify expressions in terms of functions which we would find it difficult if not (practically) impossible to spell out in terms of explicit rules.

66.     The above discussion of 'means' is but the entering wedge for the resolution of our problem. It provides the essential clues, but its significance is not yet manifest. For there are other ways of making meaning statements than by the use of 'means'. And it is these other ways which have generated much of the confusion and perplexity which are characteristic of the "theory of meaning."

67.     Thus consider

(4) '*Dreieckig*' (in German) *stands for* triangularity.

---

[19] It is, of course, an over-simplification to speak of "the" function of a certain expression in a given language. Classifications are always relative to a purpose. Various devices can be used to make it clear *which* functions of the word which is used to form an illustrating sortal are serving as criteria for its application. As was pointed out in note 15 above, the use of illustrating sortals is flexible, criteria of application shifting with context and purpose. Thus the mere fact that a token is classified as a •simultaneous• (said to mean*simultaneous*)need not pin it down to either the function of 'simultaneous' in a relativistic corpus or its function in a classical corpus. On the other hand the context of classification *may* so pin it down. In the former case, 'is a •simultaneous•' (means *simultaneous*) would be a generic functional classification and would have as its species 'is a relativistic •simultaneous•' (means *simultaneous* (relativistic)) and 'is a classical •simultaneous•' (means *simultaneous* (classical)).

[20] It should be clear from the argument of the preceding chapter that the copula 'is' does not stand for an "ontological *nexus*" (exemplification). Notice that from my point of view Bergmann is (mis-)perceptive but consistent when he treats meaning as a nexus. See his "Intentionality," in *Semantica,* Rome 1955, reprinted in *Meaning and Existence,* Madison 1960, 3-38.

According to appearances (surface grammar) the following seem to be the case: (a) 'Triangularity' is a name. (b) It refers to a non-linguistic entity. (c) *Stands for* is a relation which, given the truth of (4), holds between a linguistic and a nonlinguistic entity. I shall argue that (a), (b) and (c) merely *seem* to be the case and that, contrary to the general opinion, to "countenance" statements like (4) is *not* to commit oneself to a Platonistic ontology.

68.    The point grows directly out of our previous account of 'means' sentences. For there we encountered three ideas which can be put to good use: (a) 'Means' is a specialized form of the copula. (b) What follows 'means' is to be construed as a meta-linguistic sortal. (c) The subject of a 'means' statement is a meta-linguistic distributive singular term. To put these ideas to work in the analysis of (4), all we need to do is to construe 'triangularity' as a meta-linguistic distributive singular term, and 'stands for' as another (and more interesting) specialized copula.

69.    Consider the following sentence, which is of a kind to which logicians have paid little attention

(5) The pub is the poor man's club.

How are we to understand the copula 'is'? Only a most superficial reading would take (5) to be a statement of identity. Surely we have here a statement involving two distributive singular terms formed, respectively, from the sortals 'pub' and 'club'. It has the form

(6) the $K_1$ is the $\varphi K_2$

and is roughly equivalent to

(5$^1$) Pubs are poor men's clubs.

70.    I propose, therefore, that we read (4) as

(4$^1$) The *'dreieckig'* is the German •triangular•

which transforms into

($4^2$) '*Dreieckig*'s are German •triangular•s

or, which is the same thing,

($4^3$) '*Dreieckig*'s (in German) are •triangular•s.

71.    According to this interpretation, (4) is simply another way of doing what is done by (3), i.e., giving a functional classification of certain inscriptions belonging to the German language. What is the point of having this second way? The answer is simple: because *this* way of doing the job relates the classification to the truth context,

(7) Triangularity is true of a

which tells us, in first approximation, that

(8)    Expressions consisting of a •triangular• appropriately concatenated with an •a• are true.

72.    In general, I suggest that so-called nominalizing devices which when added to expressions, form corresponding abstract singular terms, thus '–ity', '–hood', '–ness', '–tion', 'that...', etc., are to be construed as quoting contexts which (a) form meta-linguistic functional sortals and (b) turn them into distributive singular terms.

73.    Abstract singular terms formed by the use of these quoting devices frequently contain roots which are familiar to the cognoscenti but are not generally accessible. 'Triangularity' wears its reference to the function of the predicate 'triangular' on its sleeve. To interpret

'—' (in L)[21] stands for triangularity,

---

[21] The language L may, of course, be English.

one need only rehearse the semantic functioning of 'triangular' in our language.
74.     But such direct illumination is not provided, save to the scholar, by

'—' (in L) stands for animosity.

To serve its purpose as meaning statement, the latter must itself be translated into the hearer's (or reader's) dialect. The most useful way to do this is by the use of one (or more)[22] constructions of the form 'being φ', thus, perhaps,

'—' (in L) stands for (the state of) being antagonistic.

75.     Notice that such modifiers as 'the state of', 'the quality of', 'the condition of', and 'the event of' which precede 'being φ' are simply more generic functional classifications of predicative roles.
76.     Thus 'triangularity' merely *looks* (to the eye bewitched by a certain picture) to be a name. It merely *looks* as though it referred to something non-linguistic. Applying to expressions in *any* language which do a certain job, its *inter*-linguistic reference is confused with a *non*-linguistic reference. Again 'stands for' merely *seems* to stand for a relation. It is, as 'means' proved to be, a specialized form of the copula.

## VIII

77.     Just as '–ity', '–hood', and '–ness' are quoting devices which form semantical sortals out of predicates, so 'that' is a quoting device which forms semantical sortals out of sentences. Schematically,

that $(2 + 2 = 4)$ = the •2 + 2 = 4•.

78.     Just as

'*rot*' (in G) means *red*

---

[22] Remember the points about classification and similarity of meaning (function) stressed in previous footnotes.

is to be reconstructed as

    '*rot*'s (in G) are •red•s,

so

    '*Es regnet*' (in G) means *it rains*

is to be reconstructed as

    '*Es regnet*'s (in G) are •it rains•s.

79.    Again, just as

    '*rot*' (in G) stands for redness

is to be reconstructed as

    '*rot*' is the German •red•

and, hence, as

    '*rot*'s (in G) are •red•s,

so

    '*Es regnet*' (in G) stands for (the proposition) that it rains

is to be reconstructed as

    '*Es regnet*' is the German •it rains•

and, hence, as

'*Es reg net*'s (in G) are •it rains•s.

80.    Once again the question arises 'Why are there *two* semantical statement forms, involving the pseudo-predicates 'means' and 'stands for' respectively, which have, in the last analysis, the same reconstruction?'

81.    The answer is that the 'stands for' rubric fits neatly with contexts associated with the concept of truth. This is not true of the 'means' rubric. Thus,

'*a ist dreieckig*' (in G) means *a is triangular*

culminates in a use of 'a is triangular' which does not have the clear cut surface grammar of a referring expression, though the context

--- is true

is a predicative one and calls for a subject which does have this surface grammar.

82.    Consequently, if we try to capture our intuitions concerning the relation of "truth" to "meaning" by the conjunction

'*a ist dreieckig*' (in G) means *a is triangular* and *a is triangular* is true,

we find a surface grammar which is not even ostensibly perspicuous.

83.    On the other hand,

'*a ist dreieckig*' (in G) stands for (the proposition) that a is triangular

culminates in an expression which does have the surface grammar of a singular referring expression and is therefore suited to the truth contexts, thus

that a is triangular is true.

84.    As a result, the conjunction

'*a ist dreieckig*' (in G) stands for (the proposition) that a is triangular and that a is triangular is true has an (ostensibly) perspicuous surface grammar. That its deep structure is

'*a ist dreieckig*'s (in G) are •a is triangular•s and •a is triangular•s are true

which is also the deep structure of

'*a ist dreieckig*' (in G) means *a is triangular* and *a is triangular* is true

illustrates the subtlety with which surface grammar reconciles pressures which arise from the fact that however intimate the connection between meaning and truth, the *immediate* function of meaning statements requires a surface grammar which highlights the rehearsing *use* of expressions, whereas the *immediate* function of truth statements requires a surface grammar of *reference* and *predication*. From this point of view, 'stands for' statements serve to link the 'meaning' statements with which they are logically equivalent to the context of truth.

85.    To say that

'*dreieckig*' (in G) stands for triangularity

is to say (in a unique way) that 'dreieckig' does the job in German which is done in our language by 'triangular'. In a Jumblese language, however, i.e., one which contains no predicative auxiliary expressions, there would be no expression which does this job. Thus there would be no true statement of the form

'——' (in J) stands for triangularity
i.e.,
'——'s (in J) are •triangular•s.

86.    On the other hand, since the basic job of 'triangular's in English PMese is to give individual constants the character of being concatenated with a *triangular*, thus,

triangular a,

we can say that the job done by

individual constants which are concatenated with a *triangular*

is done in Jumblese by (for example)

individual constants which are in bold face.

Thus boldface individual constants would be the Jumblese linguistic representatives of triangular things.

87.    In other words, although nothing in Jumblese would *stand for triangularity,* it would nevertheless be true that

boldface 'a' (in J) stands for (the proposition) that a is triangular

i.e.,

boldface 'a's (in J) are •a is triangular•s.

88.    Against this background, how are such statements as

That a is triangular is true

to be explicated? Clearly the first step is to reconstruct the latter as

•a is triangular•s are true.

89.    But how is the predicate 'true' itself to be explicated? What does one say when one says that expressions in any language, which do (to a relevant extent) the job done in our language by 'a is triangular's, are true?

90.    The clue is to be found in the fact that the job of 'a' is to be the linguistic representative of *a*, and the job of individual constants which are concatenated with an 'is triangular' is to be the linguistic representatives of triangular things. These jobs reflect some of the ought-to-bes which govern the process of world story construction which is the core function of language.

91.    This connection of features of 'a is triangular' with ought-to-bes suggest that the truth of 'a is triangular' is itself an ought-to-be.

92.     The idea that where 'a's are the linguistic representatives (in L) of *a*, 'a's which are concatenated with an 'is triangular' *correctly* depict *a* (in L) and belong in L's world story if and only if *a* is triangular will be explored in greater detail in the following chapter.

93.     I have argued that, in general,

'—' (in L) is true

has the sense of

'—'s in (in L) are semantically assertible

where 'semantically assertible' means *correctly* tokenable in accordance with the semantical rules of L—as contrasted with the correctnesses of rhetoric and taste.

94.     If 'true in L' has as its generic sense *semantically correct sentence of L*[23] the specific varieties of truth-in-L, e.g., *true atomic sentence of L*, would arise from the varieties of criteria for the semantical assertibility of specific kinds of sentence in L. At the bottom of this tree of correctness would be the criteria for the correctness of individual sentences such as 'a is triangular' and of sentences formed from them by such logical operations as negation, disjunction and quantification.

95.     Obviously 'true' does not mean the same as either 'known to be true' or 'probably true'. Thus 'correctly assertible' does not mean the same as 'assertible with good reason or warrant'. Semantic and epistemic oughts must be handled with the same care as that involved in distinguishing (and relating) the various senses in which an action can be said to be morally suitable.

96.     It is the connection of the truth of atomic empirical statements with the ought-to-bes of linguistic representation which accounts for the fact that

'a is red' (in L) is true

---

[23] Of course there is a weaker sense of semantically correct in which a well-formed but false sentence can be said to be semantically correct. It might therefore by intuitively more plausible to explicate truth in terms of semantical correctness *and success*. But to follow up this aspect of semantical ought-to-bes would call for a finer-grained botanizing of normative concepts than time and space permit.

*because*

a is red.

97.    Who would suppose that

'a' is the linguistic representative (in L) of *a*

*because*

xLRy (in L) =$_{df}$ (x = 'a' & y = a) or (x = 'b' & y = b) or...

even though it were true that

x is the linguistic representative (in L) of y = xLRy?

98.    A truth condition in what might be called the *ordinary* sense of 'condition' is something with reference to which the truth of a sentence can be *explained*, much as a *goodness* condition is something with reference to which the goodness of something, e.g., an apple, can be *explained*. A recursive structure of T-biconditionals pertaining to a formalization L′ of a language L no more gives the *sense* of 'true in L', than 'xLRy (in L′)' gives the sense of 'x is the linguistic representative (in L) of y', even though

x is true (in L) ≡ x is T (in L′).

### IX

99.    The above remarks take one to the foothills of the Everest which is the task of constructing a theory of truth capable of handling the puzzles and paradoxes in which the subject abounds. I shall certainly not attempt to scale this Everest on the present occasion. I shall prudently limit myself to the foothills in the hope that the geology of the summit as glimpsed along the way will cohere with the geological strata uncovered by the previous arguments.

100.    Thus the next thing to note is that the concept of truth is the head of a

family of what might be called alethic concepts: exemplification, existence, standing in (a relation), (an event's) taking place, (a state of affairs) obtaining, being in (a state), and many others.

101.   The close relation of alethic concepts to that of truth can be illustrated by the following equivalences

a exemplifies f-ness       ≡   that it is f is true of a
                           ≡   that a is f is true ≡ a is f

a exists ≡   a exemplifies some attribute ≡   something is true of a ≡ $(\exists f)fa$

f-ness is realized       ≡   something exemplifies f-ness
                         ≡   that it is f is true of something   ≡   $(\exists x)fx$

A coronation of George V took place   ≡   that he is crowned was true of George V
                                      ≡   that George V is crowned was true
                                      ≡   that George V was crowned is true
                                      ≡   George V was crowned.

102.   I have discussed some of these alethic concepts and the puzzles which have been generated by misunderstanding them in a number of places.[24] In this chapter I shall concentrate on the supposed ontological nexus or tie of exemplification.

103.   It should come as no surprise when I claim that

a exemplifies triangularity

does not assert that one object, a, stands in a relation (or nexus) to another, triangularity. The statement in question is to be reconstructed rather as

That it is triangular is true of a

which is logically equivalent to

---

[24] See, for example, "Time and the World Order," in H. Feigl, M. Scriven and G. Maxwell (eds.) *Minnesota Studies in the Philosophy of Science*, Vol. III, Minneapolis, 1963; "Actions and Events" (AAE) [reprinted as chapter 10 in EPH], and "Metaphysics and the Concept of a Person" (MP) [reprinted in KTM].

That a is triangular is true

i.e.,

•a is triangular•s are semantically assertible.

104.   Thus, although 'true of' is an extensional context in the sense that if a = b, then whatever is true of a is true of b, it is nevertheless a quoting context and has the sense of

INDCON⌐•is•⌐•triangular• is true (•a•/INDCON)

where 'INDCON' is a non-illustrating meta-linguistic sortal which applies to individual constants, and the statement tells us that expressions which consist of an INDCON concatenated with an •is triangular• are true in case the INDCON in question is an •a•.

105.   As before, we need to highlight the difference between the truth condition *proper* of the truth that a is triangular and truth functionally equivalent states of affairs. The former is a matter of linguistic representatives in a *primary* sense. For, given that

a = the x such that x is *over there*

the expression 'the x such that x is *over there*' could be said to be in a *derivative* sense a linguistic representative of a.[25]

106.   We have seen that it is with respect to the semantical ought-to-bes of a language that we can distinguish between equivalences which *explain*, thus

'a is triangular' (in L) is true   ≡   a is triangular

and equivalences which do not, thus

'a is triangular' (in L) is true   ≡   the x such that x is over there is triangular.

---

[25] It is at this point that Kripke's distinction between rigid and non-rigid designators becomes relevant.

107.   Thus we might distinguish between

That it is triangular is true *primarily* of a,

i.e.,

a *as such*[26] exemplifies triangularity

and the weaker

That it is triangular is true *of* a,
i.e.,
a *(sans phrase)* exemplifies triangularity.

108.   One might be tempted to define 'true of' in terms of '*primarily* true of' in such a way that

That it is triangular is true of x $=_{df}$ ($\exists$y) y = x and that it is triangular is *primarily* true of y.

But while the surface structure of this suggestion is acceptable, it is not philo-sophically perspicuous since it obscures the fact that all alethic predicates are ultimately to be introduced in terms of the basic use of 'true' as in

That a is triangular is true,
i.e.,
•a is triangular•s are true.

109.   Thus the definition for which we are looking will quantify not at the object language level but at the meta-linguistic level. To satisfy this requirement the weaker context

---

[26] 'As such' like '*qua*' has an important use in a variety of contexts. Here I am using it in a "negative" sense in which it implies that 'a' is a rigid designator.

That it is triangular is true of the x such that x is *over there*

might be reconstructed as

($\exists$ INDCON) INDCON ME •the x such that x is *over there•* and INDCON⁻•is triangular• is true

where it is understood that the INDCON in question is a representative *in the primary sense* of an object.[27] The symbol 'ME' abbreviates 'is materially equivalent to', where to say that one INDCON is materially equivalent to another is to say that any true context in which one occurs remains true if replaced by the other. Thus,

INDCON$_i$ ME INDCON$_j$

is the meta-linguistic counterpart of an object language identity statement, thus

$a = b$

and must be carefully distinguished from the object language

$x = y \equiv (f)fx \equiv fy.$[28]

110.   The upshot of these remarks is to reinforce the contention of the preceding chapter that to yield its full measure of ontological insight the strategy of treating predicative expressions as auxiliary expressions should be applied at the level of empirical subject predicate statements, rather than merely at the level of exemplification statements.

111.   At the latter level a proper use of the strategy would invoke a principle to the effect that

---

[27] For a more detailed account of the distinctions necessary to cope with quantification into quotation contexts, see my "Reply to Quine" (RQ) in *Synthese*, 26, 1973 [reprinted as chapter 8 in EPH].

[28] These and related issues are canvassed in a letter to Michael Loux which is printed as an appendix to this volume.

One can only say that a exemplifies f-ness by placing 'a' and 'f-ness' in a dyadic relation

and argue that

a exemplifies f-ness

itself satisfies this principle by placing an 'a' and an 'f-ness' in the dyadic relation of having an 'exemplifies' between them.

112.   But here one must be careful, for what is an 'exemplifies'? Is it a token of a sign design which has no *independent* semantical function? That was the crux of our treatment of ordinary predicates as auxiliary expressions.

113.   Of course, in the fullness of ordinary language, expressions which from the point of view of the problems with which we are dealing are auxiliary expressions and have no independent semantical function are involved in other modes of semantical functions. Thus 'adjoins' is a tensed verb and as such makes an important semantical contribution to sentences in which it occurs. How such functions would be performed in a Jumblese dialect is an important topic for investigation. The reader should bear this in mind and think in terms of a regimented PMese which abstracts from these other modes of semantical functioning. Otherwise one's intuitive sense of the richness of the roles played by unregimented predicates will render implausible the thesis that *as predicates* they are auxiliary expressions.

114.   I have argued that

a adjoins b

places an 'a' and 'b' in the dyadic relation of having an *adjoins* between them. What is the difference between having an *adjoins*—a certain design—between them and having an 'adjoins' between them? The difference is, of course, that the latter implies that what is between the 'a' and 'b' is performing a certain semantical function as an expression in the language.

115.   But what function? On our interpretation (and with the qualification stressed in the preceding paragraphs but one), it is simply that of placing an 'a' an

a 'b' in a *convenient* kind of dyadic relation—as contrasted, for example, with\

a
  b

which, in spite of its philosophical perspicuousness, places an 'a' and a 'b' in an *inconvenient* dyadic relation. Thus 'adjoins' has no independent semantical function.

116.    Thus, the semantical function of our regimented 'adjoins' is *derivative* from that of the pairs of individual constants which it relates. This functioning is a matter of a pattern (language-world and language-language) in which individual constants with an *adjoins* between them ought to occur. In our Jumblese language these same patterns would involve pairs of individual constants one of which is catacorner-left to the other one, and nothing in Jumblese would be doing the job done by *adjoins*.

117.    But does not *adjoins* have the semantical function of *meaning is next to*, of *standing for* juxtaposition? *Certainly*, but if the argument of this chapter is sound, *meaning* and *standing for* are *not* semantical functions.

118.    It is the right-hand side of

    *adjoins* (in E) means *is next to*
    *adjoins* (in E) stands for juxtaposition

which pinpoints the semantical function of *adjoins* as an English word. And this function is to be that of an auxiliary symbol which has the *derivative* semantical function characterized above.

119.    The point of these, I'm afraid repetitious, considerations is to prepare the way for the following challenge: A platonist who makes use of the *predicates are auxiliary expressions* strategy (see paragraphs 21-28 above) must give an explanation of the statement

    'exemplifies' (in E) stands for exemplification

which is compatible with this strategy.

120.    Thus if the platonist so interprets this truth that it ascribes an *independent*

semantical function to 'exemplifies', e.g., that of standing in a meaning nexus, the position becomes incoherent. For if

a exemplifies F

simply brings it about that an 'a' and an 'F' have an \*exemplifies\* between them, where a pair of lower case and upper case names with an \*exemplifies\* between them are the linguistic representatives of pairs of objects one of which exemplifies the other, then there simply is no entity in this ontological assay to be the term of a meaning nexus.

121.   On the other hand, if the platonist bites the bullet and accepts the idea that meaning statements are functional classifications and grants that the semantical function of 'exemplifies' is *derivative* from the semantical function of sentences in which 'exemplifies' plays the role of an auxiliary expression, he is confronted by the fact that the surface grammar of such statements as

'dreieckig' (in G) stands for triangularity

have been one of platonism's most effective weapons. To abandon the idea that 'triangularity' in *this* context is the name of an extra-linguistic entity is to lose the advantage of intuitive appeal. Nominalism no longer seems to be flying in the face of reason.

122.   A platonist must also come to terms with the fact that there is obviously a close conceptual connection between exemplification and truth. What account can he give of this fact?

123.   Remember that on his account, atomic propositions of the form 'Fx' e.g.,

Red a,

in and of themselves assert that a certain particular *exemplifies* a certain universal. For the above statement is *identical in sense* with

a exemplifies Red

differing from it only by not using an auxiliary expression.

124.   It follows that exemplification cannot be *analyzed* in terms of truth. The equivalence

a exemplifies F $\equiv$ that Fa is true

which is indeed a *necessary* one cannot be recast as

a exemplifies F $=_{df}$ that Fa is true,

for the latter would be equivalent to the absurdity

Fa $=_{df}$ that Fa is true.

125.   But, it might be argued, the platonist could capture the conceptual tie between exemplification and truth with the claim that truth is to be defined in terms of exemplification, thus

That Fa is true $=_{df}$ a exemplifies F.

But this would be equally absurd, for it would be synonymous with

That a exemplifies F is true $=_{df}$ a exemplifies F

which, as a *definition* (though not as a necessary equivalence), is incoherent.
126.   On the other hand the approach to exemplification advanced in this chapter *does* permit a definitional relationship between exemplification and truth. Furthermore, it enables one to see *why* the regress of exemplification which has haunted conceptual realists from Plato to Bradley since the discovery of the Third Man is benign. For,

a exemplifies F-ness $\equiv$ [a, F-ness] exemplify exemplification

has the deep structure

that-Fa is true $\equiv$ that-(that-Fa is true) is true

and this is as harmless as can be.

127.    It is only if one takes exemplification to be a nexus in the world that one will feel constrained to interpret

a exemplifies F-ness $\equiv$ [a, F-ness] $^2$exemplify $^1$exemplification

as warranting

a exemplifies F-ness because [a, F-ness] $^2$exemplify $^1$exemplification.

128.    My aim in this chapter has been to show that a dialectical examination of conceptual realism in the context of semantics reinforces the claim, advanced in the preceding chapter, that empirical predicates are just that, i.e., *predicates* (*not* unperspicuous names), and that although 'exemplifies' is, indeed, a predicate, the theory of predicates as auxiliary expressions, so helpful in resolving the Bradley paradox, is to be applied, in first instance, to such predicates as 'red' and 'triangular'.

X

129.    Clearly the present occasion does not permit a systematic development of the semantical theory of which the preceding is but the prelude. I can only hope that enough has been said to strengthen the claim that a naturalistic ontology must be a nominalistic ontology.

130.    Let me conclude this chapter with a few asides. Notice, to begin with, the new look of the problem of "identity conditions for attributes." Since talk about attributes is talk about linguistic "pieces," and not about platonic objects, identity means sameness of function and belongs in a continuum with similarity of function.

131.    Thus, after studying two games which use physically different materials and motions, we might decide that the two games are the "same," i.e., that we can find an abstract specification of correct and incorrect moves and positions such that it picks out for both games the moves and positions which are correct or incorrect according to their less abstractly formulated rules.

132.    And by virtue of this fact, we could say, for example, that the *Dame* of one

game is the Queen of the other. By parity of reasoning, we can say that

f-ness = g-ness if and only if the rules for •f•s are the same as the rules for •g•s.[29]

One can also make sense of the idea that bishops are more like castles than they are like knights. Indeed, we are all accustomed to making judgments of this kind: "The bowler in cricket is like the pitcher in baseball." We decide similarity of "pieces" with reference to the roles they are given by the rules.

133.  Let us now look at likeness of meaning from a somewhat different direction. Consider the familiar fact that isosceles triangularity and scalene triangularity are species of triangularity. In our framework this is spelled out as the fact that

•isosceles triangular•s

and

•scalene triangular•s

consist of a common predicate (a •triangular•) concatenated with a modifier (an •isosceles•, a •scalene•) in such a way that •triangular•s, •isosceles triangular•s, and •scalene triangular•s constitute a fragment of a system of geometrical classification.

134.  The important point is that isosceles triangularity is to be construed as (isosceles triangular)-ity, the scope of the quoting context '-ity' being indicated by the parentheses. Contrast this with the contrast between Euclidian triangularity and Riemannian triangularity. Here the scope of '-ity' is simply 'triangular'. Thus to talk about Euclidian triangularity is to talk not about

•Euclidian triangular•s

but about

---

[29] For a further development of this theme and a reply to important objections see the Appendix.

Euclidian •triangular•s,

i.e., inscriptions which function as does our word 'triangular' when it is governed by specifically Euclidian principles.

135.     Thus it is important to note that the use of the illustrating device to form functional sortals involves an important flexibility. Not all aspects of the functioning of the illustrating expression need be mobilized to serve as criteria for its application. Thus consider

Euclidian triangularity and Riemannian triangularity are varieties of triangularity.

This becomes

Euclidian •triangular•s and Riemannian •triangular•s are varieties of •triangular•.

It is clear that the functioning of the illustrating word 'triangular' which is relevant to something's being a •triangular• is a generic functioning which abstracts from the specific differences between Euclidian and Riemannian geometries.

136.     Compare

Classical negation and intuitionistic negation are varieties of negation.

Here again the context makes clear just what aspects of the functioning of the illustrating term is being mobilized by the abstract singular term into which it is built. It is our intuitive appraisal of the functional similarity of expressions in different linguistic structures which grounds our willingness to make statements of this form.[30]

137.     I have often been asked, what does one gain by abandoning such standard platonic entities as *triangularity* or *that 2 + 2 = 4* only to countenance such exotic abstract entities as *functions, roles, rules* and *pieces*. The answer is, of

---

[30] For an elaboration of this and related themes see *Science and Metaphysics*, chapters 3-5.

course, that the above strategy *abandons nothing but a picture*. Triangularity is not abandoned; rather 'triangularity' is *seen for what it is*, a meta-linguistic distributive singular term.

138.    And once the general point has been made that abstract singular terms are meta-linguistic distributive singular terms, rather than labels of irreducible eternal objects, there is no reason why one should not use abstract singular terms and categories of abstract singular terms in explicating specific problems about language and meaning. For just as talk about triangularity can be unfolded into talk about •triangular• inscriptions, so talk about any abstract entity can be unfolded into talk about linguistic or conceptual tokens.

## 5  AFTER MEANING

I

1.    The preceding account of meaning statements helps to explain how they can tempt one into holding a one-dimensional, 'Fido'-Fido, theory of meaning. For meaning statements, by their very nature, focus attention on the functional equivalence of expressions. They do not tell us *how* an expressions functions, except *indirectly*, by presenting us with another expression, with the functioning of which we are presumably familiar and giving us the task of "getting with" this functioning by a rehearsal in imagination of the patterns of inferential and noninferential transitions[1] characteristic of the latter expression.

2.    Yet, meaning statements are easily misconstrued as directly telling us the function of an expression. Thus

(Expression) means ---
(Expression) stands for ---

not only *can* be, but almost invariably *have been*, interpreted as saying that the function of a certain expression is to mean or stand for[2] such and such an entity.

3.    If, however, the argument of the preceding chapter was successful, 'means' and 'stands for' are specialized forms of the *copula*, and, hence, *meaning* and *standing for* are pseudo-functions, the surface grammar of which blinds us to the genuine functions which it is the role of meaning statements to *convey*.

---

[1] For the basics of the relevant distinctions, see SPR, chapter 11, paragraphs 1-24; also "Language as Thought and as Communication" (LTC(74)) and "Reply to Marras" (RM(84)) in EPH. In the original paper I spoke of "intralinguistic moves," influenced by the game analogy. In subsequent papers the action-theoretic implications of 'move' were discounted along the lines of the present chapter.

[2] Or 'designate' or 'denote'—or whatever semantical term is being polished for theoretical use.

## II

4.      Another source of the misunderstanding of the nature of meaning is the current stress on language as a means of communication, an emphasis which has led many philosophers to view language primarily in the perspective of action-theory. Utterances are construed as *actions* which, when successful, realize *intentions* that hearers acquire *beliefs*. An attempt is then made to construe the *meaning* of linguistic items in terms of the *conceptual content* of the standard intentions and beliefs which are involved in the acts of communication in which these items are deployed.

5.      If the aboutness or intentionality of mental states of believing and intending is taken as a primitive notion—either *absolutely* (as a metaphysical tie between thought and the world) or *relatively* (as a place holder for a complex concept to be defined in a naturalistic theory of mind)—the result is to focus attention once again on one-one correlations between linguistic and non-linguistic entities. This time, however, the correlations would be mediated by connections between (a) language and mental items (believings, intendings, etc., and their constituents) and (b) the latter and extra-mental reality. The contexts

(Expression) means ---
(Expression) stands for ---

would be treated, in effect, as shorthand for more complicated locutions of the form

(Expression) R (mental item) *and* (mental item) R' —.

6.      Now that language *is* a means of communication cannot, of course, be denied. But to pick language up by *this* handle is to run the risk of getting things upside down. For even more basic is the role of language as that *in which we think*.

7.      I have stressed for many years the primacy of the concept of the free-reined flow of linguistic behavior ("thinking-out-loud" I have called it) in a sound philosophy of mind.

8.      It is not easy to capture in a few words what I mean by 'free-reined' in this connection. A first attempt might be 'not brought about on purpose'. But this would overlook the fact that thinking-out-loud about a problem can be brought about on purpose as when, for example, one says musingly, "Let me see: How does the proof of the Pythagorean Theorem go?"

9.      We might amend the suggestion by saying 'not brought about by the intention to communicate to an audience'. But this would overlook the fact that a thinking-out-loud can be *governed* by the intention to be shared. Just as the primary form of thinking is thinking-out-loud, so the *primary* form of communication is a conversational dance.[3] The behavior of a couple dancing in the contemporary free-reined style is governed by a complex of general intentions, a fact, however, which is compatible with the free-reined character of the dance.

10.     This suggests a further refinement, 'not brought about by the intention to communicate such-and-such a specific message'. This will do for my present purposes. I need only add that the linguistic behavior must be serious (*engagée*) in the sense in which play rehearsals are not.

11.     I wrote above of the "primacy" of the concept *thinking-out-loud* in a sound philosophy of mind. This primacy is two-fold. In the first place such languaging (if I may so call it) by one who knows the language *is thinking in its own right*. Concepts pertaining to such thinking, whether fully actualized in utterance or occurring as proximate, "tip of the tongue," propensities to utter—inhibited only by a general "keep it to yourself" frame of mind—constitute the basic stratum of concepts pertaining to conceptual activity, much as concepts pertaining to the middle-sized objects of the perceptual environment constitute the basic stratum of concepts pertaining to the physical.

12.     From the perspective of this stratum, a sequence of thoughts simply is a sequence of proximate propensities to utter, where these propensities realize *as propensities* a pattern of sentences which conforms to the permissions and prohibitions which are characteristic of the language.

13.     That the imagination (using this term in a Spinozistic spirit) tends to construe unactualized *propensities to utter* as "hidden" *utterances* prepares the way for the introduction of a framework of "inner speech" episodes in which the

---

[3] Compare the transformation of 'It is hot over *here* where *I* am' into 'It is hot over *there* where *you* are' with the role of counterpart steps in ballroom dancing.

"utterances" are pruned of absurdities and enriched by the requirements of their explanatory role, e.g., those which pertain to the "speed" of thought.

14. For just as a distinction can be drawn between those concepts of the physical which pertain to the kinds, attributes and dispositions of the perceptual world and the micro-theoretical concepts which serve to enrich and revise our picture of the world, so a distinction can be drawn between a stratum of concepts pertaining to thought as publicly perceptible languagings and a superimposed stratum of concepts pertaining to thoughts as inner episodes which serves to enrich and revise our understanding of what goes on when people think—think, that is, in the sense defined by the former stratum.

15. That the second stratum defines a concept of thinking (thought$_2$) which is *other than* that of shifting propensities to think-out-loud (thought$_1$) is no more surprising than that theoretical physics defines a concept of the physical *other than* that of common sense. Nor is it surprising that concepts pertaining to thoughts$_2$ have developed in terms of analogies and disanalogies with thoughts$_1$.

16. A "physicalist" or "identity theorist" can be expected to claim that the framework of thoughts$_2$ is a schematic placeholder for the neurophysiological account of thinking which he believes to be just over the horizon. A neo-cartesian, who, like his forebears, mistakes the *functional* aspects of thoughts$_2$—their intentionality—for unique *descriptive* features, will view the framework of thoughts$_2$ as a framework of *non-physical* processes which has been developed in an attempt to understand and *explain* the distinctive features of meaningful speech. Such a neo-cartesianism might be called Explanatory Cartesianism to contrast it with the traditional doctrine of the givenness of the mental.[4]

17. Whichever of these strategies is followed, a radical mistake must be avoided if one is not to lapse into incoherence. The mistake consists in a failure to keep in mind a key feature of the relation between the two strata of concepts pertaining to thought, namely that the "languagings" of the first stratum are already *and as such* characterized by meaningfulness and intentionality. Indeed, their "semantical properties" are the model for the semantical dimension of the second stratum of concepts. If this is not steadfastly remembered, the fact that the second

---

[4] One can just as readily conceive of an Explanatory Aristotelianism, for while the latter would reject a dualism of mental and physical *substances*, it would insist on a dualism of mental and physical *processes*, the former having the non-physical descriptive character which, as in the case of cartesianism, miscategorizes the functional and rule-governed aspects of thoughts$_2$.

stratum provides an *enriched* and *more subtle* account of thinking-out-loud may be misconstrued as its being the positing of "thoughts" to be the causal antecedents of "speech."

18.     It would be as though the micro-physical processes introduced by sophisticated physical theory were construed as *causal antecedents* of physical processes as conceptualized in pre-theoretical terms. But the micro-physical processes which take place, according to theory, when salt dissolves in water do not stand to the dissolving as cause to effect. They *are* the dissolving more adequately conceived. The motions of the micro-particles which take place as a cloud moves across the sky do not cause the clouds to move; they *are* the motion of the cloud according to a finer-grained mode of conception.

19.     Similarly, the concept of thoughts$_2$ as "inner episodes" developed not to provide *causes* of thinking-out-loud, but to enable a finer-grained account of what thinking-out-loud *is*. To fail to appreciate this is to confuse the concept of verbal *behavior* in the full-blooded sense of the term with the concept of verbal "behavior" as the patterned emission of phonemes—as one might confuse the concept of a smile with that of an upward curving of the edges of the mouth, or the concept of a raising of ones hand with that of its upward motion.

20.     To put the point in terms I have used elsewhere, the "successor concept" to *thinking-out-loud* is not that of thoughts as inner episodes, but rather that of complex episodes which consist of *behavioral elements* (in the thin sense), *inner episodes* (functionally conceived) and *adumbrated processes* (presumably neurophysiological) which are physical in the minimal sense of being defined in descriptive rather than semantical terms and which (a) embody the *functions* by virtue of which they are thoughts$_2$ and (b) relate them to muscles and sense organs.

21.     To be sure, *if* we now eviscerate the original concept of thinking-out-loud by removing those aspects which pertain to its functional and rule-governed character, *then* we can appropriately think of thoughts$_2$ as causal antecedents of verbal "behavior." But to do this is, in so far forth, to lose sight of the original explanandum and to let go of Ariadne's thread in the labyrinth of the mental.

22.     To think of thoughts$_2$ as *causes* of thinking-out-loud (and the point becomes analytic when put in this way) is implicitly to eviscerate the concept of thinking-out-loud by eliminating those of its features which pertain to the ascription of such semantical properties as meaning, reference, sense, truth, and entailment. And to do this is to play into the hands of dualism—in either its neo-

Cartesian or neo-Aristotelian form—by reinforcing the idea that verbal behavior (remember the ambiguity) *as such* lacks intentionality. This easily becomes the idea that the "intentionality" of verbal behavior *consists in* its being caused by episodes which, alone, have *intrinsic* intentionality and hence, alone, are properly characterized as thoughts.

23.     The truth of the matter is rather that verbal behavior as thinking-out-loud has *intrinsic* intentionality. So, also, do the thoughts$_2$ which are, in part, conceived by analogy (and disanalogy) with thinkings-out-loud. We can, indeed, say that verbal behavior (in the *thin* sense) has intentionality because it is the expression (in a *causal* sense of this term) of inner episodes which have *intrinsic* intentionality. But we can also say that verbal behavior *in the full-blooded sense* has *intrinsic* intentionality by virtue of the functional roles it embodies. Thinking-out-loud expresses (in a *non-causal* sense of this term) meanings by virtue of *realizing* (in the theatrical sense) these roles.

24.     I began this section by suggesting that to pick language up by the handle *means of communication* is to run the risk of "getting things upside down." This danger is illustrated by the following train of thought:

> Linguistic episodes are actions pertaining to the framework of communication. Though individual linguistic actions can be performed without communicating or even intending to communicate, their dependence on this framework is shown by the fact that an adequate account of semantical concepts pertaining to linguistic episodes requires a reference to the practice of communication. Thus, to be a saying-that-p is to be the kind of utterance which would, in definable circumstances, communicate the *message* that-p. The concept of saying-that-p, therefore, involves the concepts of *intending to communicate that-p* and of *believing that-p*.
>
> Some thought episodes, e.g. noticing that-p, are essentially *non-actions*. No episode is a noticing that-p if it is directly brought about by the intention that it occur. The same is true of occurrent believings, inferrings and intendings. Since these are central to the framework of thoughts, no linguistic episodes can, as such, *be* thoughts, though they can, of course, *express* them. Thus, the concept of thinking-out-loud, on which you build your philosophy of mind, is incoherent.
>
> To understand a linguistic expression is to grasp it as the sort of thing which can be used to convey certain messages. It therefore involves having the concepts of intending and understanding. There is, therefore, no stratum of concepts pertaining to thinking which is more basic than that of *non-linguistic* episodes of believing and intending.

Semantical concepts pertaining to the connection between thoughts and things cannot correctly be construed as sophistications of a more basic stratum of semantical concepts pertaining to language. They constitute either an innate conceptual framework or one derived by abstraction from the introspective experience of mental activity.

Here, as in other areas, your metaphysical views, although doing more justice—at least in intention—to the complexities of things than traditional nominalisms and naturalisms, gets them upside down.

25.    I leave it to the reader to judge who is standing on his (or her) head.

III

26.    In the first section of this chapter I argued that the surface grammar of meaning statements takes the eye away from the holistic character of empirical meaning, the essential role played by coherence and interdependence. A simple, but not too over-simplified, example may help make this point intuitive.

27.    How does one explain the meaning of the word 'triangle', perhaps to a child who does not know how to use it? Obviously, if the child is already at home in geometrical language, one way of achieving this purpose would be by doing something like giving a definition. I say "something like" because, since the theory of language with which we are working has no commitment to what Quine has called the Myth of the Museum and has no place for the contemplation of Ideas or Essences, we can take the protean character of natural languages for granted. Thus it is sufficient for my purposes to stress that one way of explaining the meaning of the word 'triangle' is by offering an expression which is, to a high degree, functionally similar. One might, with a touch of nostalgia, try

'Triangle' means *plane figure bounded by three straight lines.*

28.    Now the procedure of finding strings of expressions which are functionally equivalent to the expression we are trying to explain obviously has its limitations. The child may simply not be "into" geometrical language at all. In any event, sooner or later one comes to words which it is either difficult or impossible to explain in *that* way.

29.    Thus, when it comes to such words as 'point', 'line', 'intersection', etc., an

essential part of explaining their meaning is by putting them through their paces in certain verbal contexts, thus in general sentences which express conceptual truths and in the corresponding sentence sequences which are marked by the signals of inference. To be sure, the child must also acquire the ability to respond to cases with the right words, but until these response patterns have been integrated with intralinguistic moves and language-departure transitions, they have no conceptual character and do not even count as labels.

30.     The misreading of means-statements as having the form

(Linguistic) means (Non-linguistic)

has only too easily combined with an appreciation of the necessity of word-object connections for empirical meaning to generate the radically false idea that word-object response patterns are the very essence of empirical meaning. One thinks of the positivistic dogma that the meaning of basic descriptive terms is constituted by such connections; that of other terms by definition chains which tie them to this primary vocabulary.

31.     In the preceding paragraphs but one, I referred to "general sentences which express conceptual truths." I want now to stress that the sentences I have in mind do not have the form of equivalences. They are not of the form

Something is a bachelor if and only if it is an unmarried adult male human.

The kind I have in mind serve the purpose served in sophisticated discourse by lawlike statements, the key feature of which is that they generate subjunctive conditionals and counterfactuals.

32.     Thus I suggest that once we get away from the functional equivalences highlighted by meaning statements and look at the actual functioning of empirical expressions *in situ*, we see that to *describe* their functions is to discuss the role of empirical expressions in perceptual reports, in inferences, and, as I shall shortly emphasize, in action.

33.     Thus one hasn't fully caught on to the functioning of the word 'red' unless one is not only prepared to respond to a red object in standard conditions with 'This is red' but is prepared to draw such inferences as,

This is red. So, it is *not* green.
This is red. So, it is *extended.*
Here is florescent lighting. So, although this looks crimson, it is probably maroon.

34.    Furthermore, it is part of the very meaning of certain predicates that they occur non-vacuously in inferences authorized by lawlike statements, thus

This needle is magnetized.
So, when free floating it points north.

35.    Let me sum up these sketchy remarks[5] by saying that the meaning or function of empirical predicates is, *in part,* to be caught up in a system of inference patterns only *some* of which—the least interesting—express functional equivalences of the kind stressed by traditional theories of meaning (with its quest for synonymy.) Far more important are the logically synthetic patterns which reflect the acceptance of lawlike sentences.

36.    So far I have been concentrating on predicative expressions. It is therefore time to note that an account of the representational function of *referring* expressions must also begin by calling attention to the dangers of equivalence models of meaning and reference. Here, also, one must avoid being bewitched by such sentences as

'Parigi' (in Italian) means Paris
'Socrates' denotes the teacher of Plato.

37.    Names, demonstratives and descriptions have quite different types of function, although each of them contributes in its own way to the notion of a representational system. These functions are by no means independent of each other. And they are not to be understood in terms of piecemeal, one-one connections between expressions and objects. This is *obvious* in the case of descriptive phrases, and it *should* be no less obvious in the case of such demonstratives as

---

[5] The approach to meaning which they epitomize was developed in a long series of papers, some of which have already been referred to. I might also mention "Inference and Meaning" (IM(22), reprinted in PPPW and "Counterfactuals, Dispositions and the Causal Modalities" (CDCM(33)).

'here', 'now' and 'this'. It might, therefore, be most useful to consider briefly the function of names.

38. The strategy which the equivalence model suggests is that of interpreting the semantical role of names in terms of functional equivalence to definite descriptions or clusters of definite descriptions. And undoubtedly some degree of similarity in function is to be found.

39. But consider the case of the origin, O, of a system of coordinates. There is a high degree of functional equivalence between 'O', supposing the coordinates of A to be (2,3) in a scale of inches, and 'the point which is 3 inches below A and 2 inches to the left of A'. But it is obvious that 'O' has a function which is not *constituted by* such functional equivalences.

40. Names of objects have a function which, like that of the point of origin of a coordinate system, is to be a *fixed center of reference*, a peg, so to speak, on which to hang descriptions. Or, to use a metaphor which points in the opposite direction, a name may be said to float on the descriptions it supports—a mutual relationship. For when I say "fixed," I certainly do not mean to imply that a system of names is immune to revision.

41. And, indeed, nothing in a representational system is, in principle, immune to revision, unless it be the purely formal or logical truths which themselves make no representational commitment. In practice, that is; in a given context of inquiry, certain revisions would be manifestly absurd.

IV

42. The obvious analogy to use in developing the idea of a representational system is that of a map, and I shall not refrain from using it, in spite of its dangers. Perhaps the most serious of these arises from the fact that for practical reasons maps are usually made to *look like* the terrain which they map. This fact make it easy to suppose that the essence of a map lies in its *similarity* to that which it maps—if not surface similarity, then esoteric similarity. I shall be taking a closer look at this mistake at a later stage of the argument.

43. Another danger lies in the fact that maps are used and, in particular, read. I have long argued that the representational features of an empirical language—a language which is "about the world in which it is used"—require the presence in the language of what might be called a schematic world story, a story which is as

much in process as the language itself and, of course, the world in which it is embedded. If, now, we construe the world story as a map and do not watch this metaphor like a hawk, we may suddenly find ourselves in absurdity.

44.    Consider the following sequence of statements:

1.  The core of an empirical language is a map.
2.  Thought is in touch with objects $O_1 ... O_n$ by virtue of using a map of these objects.
3.  Using a map involves reading it.
4.  A map is a structure of objects.
5.  Reading a map is a form of thinking.
6.  Reading a map involves being in touch with map-objects, $MO_1 ... MO_n$.
7.  So, being in touch with $O_1 ... O_n$ requires being in touch with $MO_1 ... MO_n$.
8.  And this, in turn, requires reading a map of $MO_1 ... MO_n$.
9.  And so on ...

45.    It is important to see that the problematic character of this regress does not arise of doubts concerning the idea of an infinite series of mappings. This idea is as legitimate as any which involves a concept of infinity—which is not to say that all puzzles pertaining to Cantor's paradise have been resolved. The problem is rather that the principles involved in the above train of thought generate a hierarchy of map *readings* which *cannot* have a top, yet *must* have a top, if thought is to be in touch with its objects.

46.    One is reminded of the thesis, attributed in a polemical spirit to representative theories of perception, according to which one sees objects by seeing objects which represent those objects. Somewhat closer to home, one is also reminded of the view that the brain thinks by producing and deciphering neurophysiological brain-language tokens.

47.    The truth of the matter is that the line of thought we are considering is but one more manifestation of the instrumentalist approach to language. In its previous appearance, it was the view that language is essentially a means of communication. In criticizing it, I argued that while language does, indeed, serve as an instrument, this role rests upon the existence of a noninstrumental stratum of linguistic behavior, the rule-governed patterns of which *constitute* the very meanings (role) of the linguistic items involved. It is in this stratum that the

propositional contents which become the *messages* of communication theory have their primary mode of being. It is no accident that behavior which is in its own right a *thinking-that-p* is of a kind which can appropriately be *used to communicate the message that-p.*

48.    Since there is an endemic tendency to use the phrase 'use of language' in such a way that all linguistic behavior is *using language*, perhaps we should say that there is a (somewhat paradoxical) non-instrumental sense of 'use' according to which people are *using language* even when they are engaged in free-floating thinking-out-loud. The existence of such an ambiguity would help explain the ease with which philosophers of language make what amounts to a category mistake.

49.    The same general strategy can be applied to puzzles about the map analogy. Maps are, indeed, used. They are consulted and, in particular, read. But could there not be a process which stands *to consulting* a map as thinking-out-loud to communication? Thinking-out-loud is a behavioral involvement of language more basic than communication. Might there not be a behavioral involvement of something which could appropriately be called a *linguistic map* which is more basic than the involvement in behavior which maps get by virtue of being *consulted*? Or, to put it in a different way, might there not be a non-instrumental mode of "reading" a map which gives maps their *meaning* and which stand to maps-as-instruments as *propositions* to *messages*?

50.    The expected answer to these rhetorical questions is, of course, yes. Reading maps contributes to the guidance of behavior. Thus these questions can be summed up in one big question: Might there not be a mode of map reading in which a map guides behavior without being used as an instrument to guide behavior? Or, to come to the essential point, without being an intermediate *object*? The answer to this question, we shall see, is an unequivocal yes. And to see why this is so is to have the solution of a puzzle which, in one form or another, has plagued the very concept of language (and thought) as a representational system.

51.    I shall approach the problem by means of an analogy. It belongs to that curious domain in which we describe the computer simulation of human behavior in the very language of human behavior—into which, however, a stratification has been introduced to correspond to the hierarchy of electronic systems and subsystems which are activated in the generation of computer behavior. This introduced stratification is a rich source of insight into the language into which it is "introduced." Indeed, to see the computer simulation as a *contrived* likeness of

human behavior is to be in a position to grasp the complex relations between reasons and causes, uniformities and rules. Of course where there are analogies, there are disanalogies, and the philosophical task, while brought to a sharper focus, remains as encompassing as before.

52.    Consider a smart missile which, in approaching its target, is "following a map." The incoming radar information is processed in accordance with a program to yield a map-representation of the missile's position. This map-representation is a complex of objects, but the missile does not respond to it as it responds to objects in its environment; i.e., it does not respond by "map-entry transitions," but rather by transforming the relevant features of the map-state into a *conjunction* of atomic *propositions* in a missile-cum-environment vocabulary (which may well use the same electronic sign-designs), thus preparing it for logical operations. The map-state, for example—where the center represents the missile—

becomes

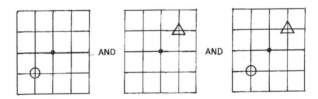

(The availability of this transformation is, we shall see, essential to the map's being, in a primary sense, a map.)

53.    These propositions belong to a more inclusive, but same-level representational system which contains an action vocabulary, thus, 'to change course', 'to fire rocket n for m seconds', 'to self-destruct', etc., as well as propositional logic, an apparatus of quantification, and a relevant part of mathematics. In addition to the "map-entry" transitions, the framework also includes representation-departure transitions from determinate imperatives to the corresponding actions.

54.    Thus, the program selects certain propositions formulated in this frame-

work to serve as "standing sentences." For example (using other sign-designs):

From any location, move towards $[x_9, y_5, z_3]$!
If at $[x_9, y_5, z_3]$, self-destruct!
If on course $C_i$ at $f[x_3, y_7, z_3]$, change course to $f'(C_i)$.
To change course to $f'(C_i)$, fire rocket n for m seconds!
etc.

The missile's program, given the state of the map, generates a sequence of intra-representation transitions which culminate for example, in the command,

Fire rocket #2 for 3 seconds!

to which, by a representation-departure transition, it responds by a 3-second firing of rocket #2.

55.     Consider, by contrast, a smart missile which is so constructed that it *consults* a map. It begins, as before, by processing incoming information. This time, however, the latter is processed in such a way that it generates a set of atomic propositions in a missile-cum-environment vocabulary, each of which ascribes a property or relation to one or more objects in the environment, including the missile.

56.     These proposition tokens are responded to, *not* by same-level intra-repre-sentation transitions culminating in the command 'Fire rocket #2 for 3 seconds!'. Rather they are responded to *as* proposition-tokens by entry-transitions into a meta-representational subsystem (semantic meta-language). This results in proposition tokens which classify the original proposition tokens in functional terms (meaning statements). This, in turn, generates a search for those elements of the representational system to which the missile's map-states belong which are descriptively synonymous with the original proposition tokens, and activates the corresponding map-state. (This activation is *included* in the finding of the synonyms, in the sense in which the map fragment illustrated in paragraph 52 is included in the conjunctive proposition into which it was transformed.)

57.     The first-level representational system of which the map-state system is a proper part *does* (as the system to which the original proposition tokens belong does *not*) include the intra-representational transition sequences (practical

reasoning) which connect map-states with commands, thus

Fire rocket #2 for 3 seconds!

58.     An examination of these two examples, both of which have been presented in a highly intuitive, catch-as-catch-can manner, should bolster the idea that the essential feature of the functioning of a map *as*, in a primary sense, a map is its location in the conceptual space of practical reasoning concerning getting around in an environment.

V

59.     In introducing the topic of maps in the previous section I referred to the view, which I have held since my earliest publications[6] that the representational features of an empirical language require the presence in the language of a schematic world story. More needs to be said about this "presence."

60.     Obviously an empirical language permits the formulation of many stories. In the first place, there are *fictions*. Such stories differ from what I am calling *the world story* of the language in that they are "bracketed" by what might be called the 'once upon a time' rubric. This has the effect of cutting them off from *practice*, i.e., removing the connection which the serious use of language has with observation and action. In this respect, to use the rubric is like stepping on the clutch of an automobile. If one is going to compare a world story with a map, one must ponder the distinction between "real" maps and "fictional" maps. One doesn't try to go places with a map of Hobbit-land.

61.     But the distinction between "real" and "fictional" maps doesn't cut deep enough. For there is a sense in which the language permits the formulation of alternative stories which are equally *engagé* in the sense that they are competitors for the status of being the accepted story of the world. What I wish to emphasize is that at any one point in this competitive process, the living language involves a *commitment* to *one* world story, however schematic and fragmentary[7]. This commitment, however, is provisional. The story is the ship which is being built

---

[6] See, e.g., "Realism and the New Way of Words" (RNWW(3)), reprinted, with alterations, in PPPW.

[7] The story is "schematic," not only in the sense of *gappy*, but also in the richer sense of containing sub-stories told in generic terms, i.e., by picking out *disjunctives* of sub-stories (for, the generic is, at bottom, the disjunctive).

(and, of course, re-built) by those who live on it. Much would have to be said about the social nature of the enterprise, the inter-personal aspects of epistemic values and norms. That, however, is a complex task for other occasions.[8]

62.   This (idealized) commitment of a language to one schematic story at any given stage of its development is not to be understood as a matter of the correspondence of that story to generally agreed upon beliefs, the beliefs being, so to speak, *external to* the language and the language *indifferent to* which beliefs are shared by the linguistic community. A language, in its primary mode of being, simply *is* the pattern of beliefs, inferences and intentions of whatever logical form or conceptual level which linguistic behavior (in the full-blooded sense) embodies. It is the instrumentalist conception of language which mis-construes it as a medium which is neutral as between the alternatives which are "expressible" in it.

63.   That languagings are *evoked* (in contexts) by happenings of certain kinds is a *causal* fact which is nevertheless essential to their conceptual character. This causal aspect of perceptual takings, introspective awarenesses, inferences[9], and volitions accounts for the selecting of *one* world story *rather than another* and connects the 'is' of this selecting with the rule-governed or 'ought to be' character of the language. The "presence" of this unique story at each stage in the development of the language makes possible the referential framework of names, descriptions and demonstratives and, by so doing, makes possible the exploratory activity which lead to the story's enrichment and revision.

64.   Thus, the fact that the uniformities (positive and negative) involved in language-entry, intralinguistic and language-departure transitions of a language are governed by specific ought-to-be statements in its meta-linguistic stratum, and these in turn by ought-to-bes and ought-to-dos concerning explanatory coherence, constitutes the Janus-faced character of languagings as belonging to both the causal order and the order of reasons. This way of looking at conceptual activity transposes into more manageable terms traditional problems concerning the place

---

[8] I have developed the theme of the intersubjectivity of ethical norms in a number of places, for example in Chapter 7 of SM(63). The corresponding point about epistemic norms and values is implicit in the discussion of meaning and truth in chapters 3 and 4. See also the concluding sections of "Are There Non-Deductive Logics" (NDL(73)), reprinted in EPH(94) .

[9] For a discussion of the relation between the logical and the causal aspects of inference, see "Thought and Action" (TA(59)), reprinted as Chapter 10 in EPH.

of intentionality in nature.

65.    The tension between the concept of the world story as the world story which *is* in point of fact accepted and the concept of *the* world story as that which *ought to be* accepted is a genuine one, the exploration of which takes one to the central issues of epistemology. Can one speak of a *nisus* of the *is* of languaging toward the *ought* of languaging? If reasons can be causes, might not there be *a* reason which is *the* cause and, indeed, the "final" cause of languaging? Weather and soil conditions may prevent the realization of the final cause of an acorn's development. Yet an acorn is, after all, an oak tree. Contingencies may block the road of inquiry, yet truth (adequacy of representation) abides as the *would be* of linguistic representation.[10]

## VI

66.    I lay aside these deeply metaphysical reflections to take up some matters of detail. We have seen that the concept of a world story is an *epistemic* concept, the concept of a story which is generated by (is) and required by (ought) the rule-governed involvement of a language in the world it is about. We, of course, are primarily concerned with languages which are embedded in *our* world (the world which includes *this*). Yet we can, of course, conceive of other worlds and of languages which are embedded in them. And the theory of such worlds and such languages is the place where all the classical problems of philosophy come together.

67.    One ostensibly small point may help put things in focus. The statements which make up a world story, in the relevant sense, are, of course, logically contingent. They have logically coherent contraries. If the story includes 'a is red', it might instead, as far as logic is concerned, have included 'a is green'. That it does not include the latter is a function of the total epistemic situation.

68.    Thus, the fact that both 'a is red' and 'a is green' are logically contingent and *in this sense* on a par does not mean that a is somehow neutral as between red and green. It may look like an unenlightening truism to say that if it is true that a

---

[10] For an excellent development of this theme see Jay Rosenberg's *Linguistic Representation*, Dordrecht-Holland, 1974 and also "The Elusiveness of Categories, the Archimedean Dilemma and the Nature of Man: A Study in Sellarsian Metaphysics," in *Action, Knowledge and Science* (ed. by Hector Castaneda), Indianapolis, 1975.

is red then *a is* red. But this is not the case, for it is *because* a is red that it is (semantically) correct to token 'a is red'. It is no news that not every *implication* generates an *explanation. In this respect*

2 + 2 = 4 iff 3 + 3 = 6

differs radically from

'a is red' (in L) is true iff a is red

where the latter is functioning as, in a strict sense, a T-sentence. Clearly if we construe 'iff' as a truth-functional equivalence, then the sequence

'a is red' (in L) is true iff Tom is tall
Tom is tall
*So*, 'a is red' (in L) is true

would have the same status as

'a is red' (in L) is true iff a is red
a is red
So, 'a is red' (in L) is true.

Yet in the second of these sequences the content is such that 'so' can be replaced by 'because', whereas in the first it cannot. One notices, of course, that the equivalence in the first sequence violates the T-sentence requirement that the expression in the quotes on the left be the same as (or a translation of) the expression not in quotes on the right. But though this requirement provides a *criterion* for picking out basic T-sentences, it does not give the *rationale* of this criterion, which concerns exactly the fact that a's being red *explains* why 'a is red' (in L) is true. It does so, roughly, because 'true' means semantically correct and 'a is red' belongs in the (correct) world story of our language.[11]

---

[11] Obviously, spelling this out involves all the delicate problems pertaining to the *is* and *ought* of languagings which I have mentioned, only to evade. For an attempt along these lines, see chapter 4 of SM.

## VII

69.    Ostensibly, I have been preparing the way for an account of world stories which construes them, so to speak, as world-sized, if schematic, maps[12]. What I actually propose to do, however, is offer an account which construes maps *in the ordinary sense* as limited and fragmentary parts of a world story. For to arrive at a clear understanding of what ordinary maps do is to grasp the role of world stories in the representational functioning of a language. Here, as elsewhere, primacy in the order of being fails to coincide with primacy in the order of understanding.

70.    The first step is to construe a map, in the ordinary sense, as a system of logically elementary sentences.[13] We can suppose these elementary sentences to translate into English, say, according to a straight-forward translation manual. Thus, a certain design patch in a certain place is the map's name for Chicago—as it thoughtfully indicates by placing the word 'Chicago' beside it. Not all the map's names of course, need be provided with translational clues.

71.    I will not bore you with the obvious details as to what translates into what. The crucial thing to get right is that there is a preferred direction of translation, just as there is a preferred direction of translation for a code. A code is a para-site—and so is a map. But the difference is significant. For whereas the items in a code translate into whole sentences, the items in a map translate into *both* names *and* sentences. (Here is where the theory of predication developed in Chapter 3 begins to pay off.) Thus the map fragment

Chicago              ▣


                        N
                        ↑

Urbana          •

[12] This should not, of course, be taken to mean that the maps could be *actualized* in one piece, but rather that they are sets of separately actualizable fragmentary maps which fit together.
[13] Not, of course, in the "absolute" sense of the *Tractatus*. Chicago is certainly not an absolute simple, though it is, in the relevant sense, an object.

is a matrix from which can be carved sentences which translate into 'Chicago is a metropolis', 'Urbana is a city', 'Chicago is northeast of Urbana'.

72.    The vocabulary of the map is limited. It does *not* include logical connectives, quantifiers or modalities. And, in particular, it does not include *descriptions*.

73.    On the other hand it *generates* descriptions by virtue of connections between the symbols on the map and the full-blooded language *of which it is a functioning part*. These connections enable the map symbols to participate vicariously in logical operations. Thus, although 'the highway which runs 80 miles south of Chicago in an east-west direction' is not the translation of any symbol on the map, to one who understands the map it trips readily off the tongue.

74.    A map is no mere list of names, though in a sense it consists of names. Even in the limiting case where every symbol on the map is a name, it is also more than a name. The map belongs to a Jumblese dialect.

75.    Although in certain respects a map can be compared to a code, one significant difference is that in certain respects the symbols on a map *resemble* the terrain which the map *represents*. It is important to see, therefore, that the map does not *represent* the terrain by virtue of the sheer existence of these similarities. They must play semantic roles which center around the fact that they translate into geographical sentences. The question as to which kinds of similarity are useful in that they enable he who runs to read a map belongs to a different dimension of the theory of maps.

76.    I pointed out a moment ago that the vocabulary of a map is extremely limited, lacking, for example, logical connectives. It is equally important to note that it lacks words for actions. Thus, although a map is for use in travelling, there are no words for 'to go forward', 'to turn right', etc. Thus, even if the map tells us that Chicago is north of Urbana, it is only in the language to which we translate the map that we get

> Going north-east from Urbana is going toward Chicago. If I am in Urbana and want to get to Chicago, I should first go north on Route 89.

77.    It is this fact which tells us what maps *are*. One doesn't have to actually use them to go to the places they represent in order for them to be maps, but the point of being a map is to translate into sentences which dovetail with *practical* dis-

course about getting from point A to point B.

> I am here. Here is Urbana.
> Chicago is north-east from Urbana on Route 89.
> This is Route 89.
> I will get to Chicago (and satisfy certain other conditions) *if and only if* I go
>     north on 89.
> I will go north on 89.

To which might be added:

> Chicago is a large city.
> Being in Chicago is being in a large city.
> (Given where I am) I will be in a large city tonight if and only if I am in
>     Chicago.
> Would that I were in a large city tonight.
> Would that I were in Chicago.

78.    Thus there is, from the point of view of practice, a *connection* between the symbol for Chicago and Chicago, and between symbols for large cities and large cities.

79.    And there is a connection between the fact that large cities have suburbs and the fact that a mapmaker would draw in a symbol for a suburb near the symbol for large cities, even if he had no direct information that there were such a suburb.

80.    This reference to constructing a map leads me back to the theme of constructing a world story. And after much cudgeling of the brain I can find no significantly better way of getting the point across than what I had to say on this topic in "Truth and "Correspondence"."[14] The following paragraphs are taken from the concluding section[15] of this essay.

VIII

81.    Is there no relation of picturing which relates the linguistic and the nonlin-

---

[14] TC(47), reprinted as Chapter 6 of SPR.
[15] Pp. 211-224 of SPR (paragraphs 39-77).

guistic orders and which is essential to meaning and truth?

82.    In the passages with which we have been concerned, Wittgenstein has been characterizing picturing as a relation between statements *considered as facts* and another set of *facts* which he calls the world. Roughly, he has been conceiving of picturing as a relation between facts about linguistic expressions, on the one hand, and facts about nonlinguistic objects, on the other.

83.    If we speak of a fact about nonlinguistic objects as a nonlinguistic fact, we are thereby tempted to think of facts about nonlinguistic objects as nonlinguistic entities of a peculiar kind: nonlinguistic pseudo-entities. We have seen, however, that 'nonlinguistic facts' in the sense of facts about nonlinguistic entities are *in another sense* themselves *linguistic* entities and that their connection with the nonlinguistic order is something done or to be done rather than a relation. It is the inferring from 'that-*p* is true' to '*p*'. And as long as picturing is construed as a relationship between *facts* about linguistic objects and *facts* about nonlinguistic objects, nothing more can be said.

84.    But what if, instead of construing "picturing" as a relationship between *facts*, we construe it as a relationship between linguistic and nonlinguistic *objects*? The very formulation brings a sense of relief, for in everyday life we speak of pictures of things or persons, not of facts. Roughly, one *object* or *group of objects* is a picture of another *object* or *group of objects*. Yet since objects can picture objects only by virtue of facts about them (i.e. only by virtue of having qualities and standing in relations), it may seem a quibble to insist that it is objects and not facts that stand in the picturing relation. It is not, however, a quibble, but the heart of the matter.

85.    Two preliminary remarks are in order before we develop this suggestion.

1. If picturing is to be a relation between objects in the natural order, this means that the linguistic objects in question must belong to the natural order. And this means that we must be considering them in terms of empirical properties and matter-of-factual relations, though these may, indeed must, be very complex, involving all kinds of constant conjunctions or uniformities pertaining to the language user and his environment. Specifically, although we may, indeed must, know that these linguistic objects are subject to rules and principles—are fraught with 'ought'—we abstract from this knowledge in considering them as objects in the natural order. Let me introduce the term

'natural-linguistic object' to refer to linguistic objects thus considered.

2. We must be careful *not* to follow Wittgenstein's identification of complex objects with facts. The point is a simple, but, for our purposes, a vital one. There is obviously *some* connection between complex objects and facts. Thus, if $C$ consists of $O_1$ and $O_2$ in a certain relation, then if $O_1$ and $O_2$ were not thus related, there would be nothing for '$C$' to refer to. But even if we construe the relation between the referring expression '$C$' and the fact that $O_1$ and $O_2$ are related in a certain way as tightly as possible, by assuming that the fact that $O_1RO_2$ is involved in the very sense of the referring expression, it nevertheless remains logical nonsense to say that the complex $C$ *is* the fact that $O_1RO_2$. The most one is entitled to say is that statements containing the referring expression '$C$' are, in principle, unpackable into statements about $O_1$ and $O_2$ *and that among these statements will be the statement* '$O_1RO_2$'. It is, however, the *statement* '$O_1RO_2$' that occurs in the expansion, not the *fact-expression* 'that $O_1RO_2$'. For there are two senses in which a statement can be said to be "about a fact," and these two senses must not be confused: (a) The statement contains a *statement* which expresses a true proposition. In this sense any truth function of a true statement is "about a fact." (b) It contains a fact-expression, i.e. the name of a fact, rather than a statement. Thus, 'That Chicago is large is the case' contains the fact expression 'that Chicago is large' and is "about a fact" in that radical sense which gives it a meta-linguistic character.

86.    This point is important, for if statements about complex objects were "about facts" in the sense of containing fact expressions, then, granting the meta-linguistic status of facts, the statement

   $C$ pictures $y$

where $C$ is a complex natural-linguistic object, would have the form

   That-$p$ pictures $y$.

Thus, while ostensibly referring to a complex natural-linguistic object, '$C$' would actually refer to the statement which describes its complexity, and statements ostensibly to the effect that certain natural-linguistic objects are pictures of other objects in nature would only ostensibly be about *natural-linguistic* objects in the sense we have defined and would actually be about statements in the full sense which involves the conception of norms and standards.

87.　That if complex objects were facts, only simple nonlinguistic objects could be pictured is a further consequence, which would lead to the familiar antinomy of absolute simples that must be there and taken account of if language is to picture the world, but of which no examples are forthcoming when a user of the language is pressed to point one out. Both of these difficulties are short-circuited by the recognition that complexes are not facts.

88.　But we have at best taken the first step on a road which may lead nowhere. For granted that there are complex natural-linguistic *objects* to do the picturing, what do they picture, and how do they do it?

89.　Let me begin by commenting on a feature of Wittgenstein's treatment of picturing which, as I see it, contains the key to the answer, but which he put to the wrong use by tying it too closely to the

　　　fact pictures fact

model. For, although this model enables him to make a sound point about the logical form of elementary statements, it loses the specific thrust of the idea that whatever else language does, its central and essential function, the *sine qua non* of all others, is to enable us to *picture* the world in which we live. It was, indeed, a significant achievement to show that it is $n$-adic configurations of referring expressions that represent $n$-adic states of affairs. But of itself this thesis throws no light on the crucial question: What is there about *this specific $n$-adic* configuration of referring expressions that makes the configuration say that the items referred to are related in *that specific $n$-adic* way? One is tempted to say that the connection between linguistic configurations and nonlinguistic configurations (i.e. between predicates and properties) is simply conventional, and let it go at that.

90.　From this standpoint, the difference between a *map* and a verbal description in terms of elementary statements is the difference between a convention that represents $n$-adic relationships of size and location by $n$-adic spatial configurations of referring expressions and one that represents these $n$-adic relationships by $n$-adic configurations of referring expressions without requiring that they be $n$-adic *spatial* configurations. And, indeed, when Wittgenstein contrasts maps as pictures that are *both spatial* and *logical* pictures with statements which are *logical* pictures but not spatial pictures, he appears to be committing himself to the view that the only *essential* feature of the picturing he has in mind is that $n$-adic atomic facts be pictured by $n$-adic configurations of names.

91.     I hope to show, on the other hand, that the analogy between statements and cartographical facts, instead of being contracted along the above lines, requires to be expanded. The first point I want to make, however, may seem to strike at the very heart of the map analogy. For it is that what we *ordinarily* call maps are logical pictures only in a parasitical way. Wittgenstein himself emphasizes that a logical picture is such only by virtue of its existence in the space of truth operations. Thus, the fact that a certain dot (representing Chicago) is between two other dots (representing, respectively, Los Angeles and New York) can say that Chicago is between Los Angeles and New York only because it is connected, by virtue of certain general and specific conventions, with the statement 'Chicago is between Los Angeles and New York'. For only with respect to statements such as the latter do we actually carry on such logical operations as negation, alternation, conjunction, and quantification. The cartographically relevant fact that the one dot is between the other two is the counterpart of the statement viewed as a triadic configuration of names. It is, however, only on the latter configuration that we perform the logical operations which are as essential to its being a statement as the fact that it is a configuration. Furthermore, even if we did perform truth operations directly on cartographical configurations, a map language for spatial relationships could exist only as a small part of a more inclusive universe of discourse, and the problem recurs: Is there anything in common between what *all* elementary statements do and the sort of thing that map configurations do, over and above the feature summed up in the slogan that an $n$-adic configuration of names pictures an $n$-adic configuration of objects?

92.     Needless to say, my answer is in the affirmative. And if, as I have suggested, the key to the answer lies in the substitution of the schema

[natural-linguistic objects] $O_1'$, $O_2'$,...,$O_n'$ make up a picture of [objects] $O_1$, $O_2$,...,$O_n$ by virtue of such and such facts about $O_1'$, $O_2'$,...,$O_n'$

for the Tractarian schema

Linguistic fact pictures nonlinguistic fact,

the account I am going to sketch nevertheless preserves in a modified way the Wittgensteinian theme that it is configurations of names that picture configurations of objects. For, to anticipate, the natural-linguistic objects which, by virtue of standing in certain matter-of-factual relationships to one another and to these nonlinguistic objects, constitute a picture of them in the desired sense, are the linguistic counterparts of nonlinguistic *objects* (*not* facts), and it is not too misleading to speak of them as 'names'. To add that it is a system of elementary *statements* (*qua* natural-linguistic objects) that is the picture is to draw upon Wittgenstein's insight that the occurrence of an elementary statement is to be construed as the occurrence *in a certain manner* of the names of the objects referred to.

93.　Let me emphasize, however, that, in my account, the *manner* in which the "names" occur in the "picture" is not a conventional symbol for the *manner* in which the objects occur in the world, limited only by the abstract condition that the picture of an $n$-adic fact be itself an $n$-adic fact. Rather, as I see it, the manner in which the names occur in the picture is a projection, in accordance with a fantastically complex system of rules of projection, of the manner in which the objects occur in the world. I hasten to add, however, that in my opinion the germs of the account I am about to offer are present in the *Tractatus*, that jewel box of insights, though submerged by the translation themes I have attempted to disentangle in the previous sections.

94.　In the following argument I shall draw heavily on a principle which I shall simply formulate and apply without giving it the defence it requires, relying, instead, on its intuitive merits. Before I state it, let me emphasize that my argument involves neither a naturalistic reduction of 'ought' to 'is' nor an emotivist denial of the conceptual character of the meaning of normative terms. It will also be remembered that, although I am making my points in connection with overt discourse, I believe that they can be extended by analogy to thoughts (in the sense of acts of thought).

95.　The principle is as follows: Although to say of something that it *ought* to be done (or *ought not* to be done) in a certain kind of circumstance is not to say that *whenever* the circumstance occurs it *is* done (or *is not* done), the statement that a person or group of people think of something as something that ought (or ought not) to be done in a certain kind of circumstance entails that *ceteris paribus* they actually *do* (or refrain from doing) the act in question whenever the circumstance occurs. I shall leave the phrase 'ceteris paribus' without unpacking it, and I shall put the principle briefly as follows: Espousal of principles is reflected in uniformities of performance. I shall not attempt to analyse what it is to espouse a principle, nor shall I attempt to explicate the meaning of normative terms. I am not claiming that to *follow* a principle, i.e. act on principle, is identical with exhibiting a uniformity of performance that accords with the principle. I think that any such idea is radically mistaken. I am merely saying that the espousal of a principle or standard, *whatever else it involves*, is characterized by a uniformity of performance. And let it be emphasized that this uniformity, though not the principle of which it is the manifestation, is describable in matter-of-factual terms.

96.        The importance of this principle for my purposes may perhaps be appreciated if one reviews the variety of respects in which linguistic performances can be said to be "correct" or "incorrect." Obviously many of these respects are irrelevant to our problem. The correctnesses and incorrectnesses with which we are concerned are those which pertain to the logical syntax of basic statements and to what I shall call "observation contexts." In what follows, I shall assume that elementary propositions and only elementary propositions are always spontaneously thought *out loud*. This, of course, leaves a great deal of thinking to be done "in the head." My problem is to see whether, on certain idealized assumptions, a mode of picturing can be defined with respect to overt discourse that might then be extended to acts of thought in their character as analogous to statements in overt discourse.

97.        The uniformities to which I am calling particular attention fall into two categories:

1. Statement-statement. These are uniformities that correspond at the overt level to espoused principles of inference. To characterize these uniformities presupposes, of course, that they involve verbal patterns that conform to the "formation rules" of the language.

2. Situation-statement. These are uniformities of the kind illustrated by a person who, in the presence of a green object in standard conditions, thinks, roughly, 'Green here now' and, hence, on our assumption, makes spontaneously the corresponding statement.

98.    Important distinctions are to be drawn within both kinds of uniformity. Furthermore, a more elaborate discussion, pointed in the direction of a theory of the mutual involvement of thought and action, would require mention of a third category of uniformities, involving a transition from statement to situation, as when a person says 'I shall take a step to the right' and proceeds to do so. This would require a discussion of the force of the word 'shall' and of the sense in which 'I shall do *A* here and now' includes the statement 'I am about to do *A* here and now'. I have touched on these topics elsewhere.[16] For my present purposes, however, I can safely assume that the "volitions" that culminate in overt action, whether verbal or non-verbal, do not themselves find overt expression.

99.    Now it is familiar fact that Hume was wobbly about the distinction between mental episodes that are thoughts that-*p* and images. It is, perhaps, equally familiar that he could do this without obvious absurdity because he simultaneously treated impressions as though they were *knowings*, e.g. *seeings that-p*. To have the impression of a red object is to see *that* a red item is in a certain place in the visual field. By contrast, to have an "idea" of a red item is to *think*, rather than to *see*, while to have a "vivid idea" is to *believe in*, rather than to *merely think of*, a certain state of affairs.

100.    Thus, Hume's terminology does enable him to do a measure of justice to important distinctions. And, by reminding you of certain characteristic doctrines, I may, perhaps, be able to lay the foundation for the view I wish to propose. The Hume I want you to consider, however, is the Hume who believes that our "perceptions" are "likenesses" of states of affairs in a public spatiotemporal world. Thus, an "impression" of lightning is a "likeness" of the occurrence of a flash of lightning, and an "impression" of thunder a "likeness" of the occurrence of a clap of thunder. Of course, for Hume the likeness in question is a conflation of the "likeness" (however it is to be construed) that a sensation has to its external cause

---

[16] For a systematic discussion of the interconnections among situation-statement, statement-statement, and statement-situation uniformities as they pertain to object languages and meta-languages, see ch. 11, SPR.

and the "likeness" we are seeking to explicate, between an elementary *act of thought*, or, in terms of the device we shall use, an elementary linguistic inscription, and an event in nature.

101.   Now Hume lays great stress on the theme that *uniformities* relating perceptible events in nature tend to be reflected in *uniformities* in our "ideas" of the lightning-thunder sequence, for instance, in an idea-of-lightning—idea-of-thunder sequence. And, of course, he speaks of a case of the latter sequence in which the prior "perception" of lightning is an "impression" or "vivid idea" as an inference culminating in a belief about thunder. That Hume's account of inference is as confused and inadequate as his account of impressions and ideas is a point on which I shall not dwell. My concern is rather with the fact that by concentrating his attention on the case where the inference is, in effect, of the form

Lightning now.
So, Thunder shortly.,

he obscures the distinction between the dates of the acts of thought and the dates of the lightning and thunder that the thoughts are about. This is not unrelated, of course, to the fact that Hume finds it difficult to account for the reference of a present idea to a prior event.

102.   But, whatever the flaws in his argument, Hume put his finger on an essential truth, which, glimpsed now and then by his successors, was invariably overwhelmed by the other ingredients of the classical correspondence theory of truth. What Hume saw, put in a terminology reasonably close to his own, was that "natural inference" supplements "recall" and "observation" to generate a growing system of "vivid ideas," which constitutes a "likeness" (sketchy though it may be) of the world in which we live.

103.   On the other hand, by failing to do justice to the propositional form of what he calls "ideas" and by failing to take into explicit account the fact that the "subjects" of these propositional ideas are individuated by virtue of the spatiotemporal relationships in which they stand, he cut himself off, as we have seen, from giving an explicit account of the difference between the inferences:

Lightning now.                                        Lightning yesterday at 10 a.m.
                                       and

So, Thunder shortly.                   So, Thunder yesterday at 10:01.

Hume's blurring of the distinction between thoughts and images permits him to assume that natural inference not only is successive *as inference*, but must concern events that are successive. This rules out the inferences:

Smoke here yesterday at 10 a.m.
So, Fire here yesterday at 10 a.m.

and, of course,

Thunder now.
So, Lightning a moment ago.

Obviously, Hume's theory of natural inference must be extended to cover these cases.

104.    Again, in developing his form of the classical doctrine that the mind knows the world by virtue of containing a "likeness" of it, Hume assumes, without careful explication, that the "perception" of a configuration of objects is a configuration of 'perceptions". This principle, though sound at the core, involves difficulties enough when 'perception' is taken in the sense of 'sensation or image'. It poses even greater problems when 'perception' is taken in the radically different sense of *propositional act of thought*. Yet it is central to Hume's conception of the mind as building, through observation, recall, and natural inference, a system of "vivid ideas" which pictures (schematically) its world (including itself). For this system, as it exists at any one time, represents events by "ideas" which are "like" them and matter-of-fact relationships between events by "like" matter-of-fact relationships between the corresponding "ideas".

105.    Our problem, of course, is how this "likeness" is to be construed, if the propositional character of the "idea" is taken seriously; that is to say, if we are to preserve the essence of Hume's contention, while avoiding his mistake of thinking of "ideas" as likenesses in the sense of duplicates. This essence is the contention that the "likeness" between elementary thoughts and the objects they picture is definable in matter-of-factual terms as a likeness or correspondence or isomorphism between two systems of objects, each of which belongs in the natural order.

106.    What matter-of-factual relationships has our previous discussion made available? In the first place there are the uniformities or constant conjunctions involved in the connection of language with environment in the observational situations. Here it is essential to think of these uniformities as a matter of responding to objects with *statements* rather than by referring expressions, thus to a green object with 'This here now is green'. This point remains, even though, from a more penetrating point of view, this statement is a referring expression.[17]

107.    Let us suppose, therefore, that observation reports have the forms illustrated by

    This here now is green
    This is one step to the right of that
    This is one heartbeat after that

and let us imagine a super-inscriber who "speaks" by inscribing statements in wax and is capable of inscribing inscriptions at an incredible rate, indefinitely many "at once." It must not be forgotten, however, that he is a thinker as well as an inscriber and thinks far more thoughts than he expresses by inscriptions.

108.    Now, whenever the inscriber sees that a certain object in front of him is green, or one step to the right of (or to the left of) another, or experiences that one happening is a heartbeat later than another, he makes the corresponding inscription. We must also imagine, as we have in effect done already, that the inscriber has a system of coordinates metrically organized in terms of steps and heartbeats and that he knows how to measure and count. And we shall suppose that he uses a "coordinate language" in which names are ordered sets of numerals, three for space, one for time, which are assigned to events on the basis of measurement. Let us further suppose that the inscriber continuously inscribes statements of the form

    1=now
    2=now

---

[17] The temptation to think of the report in question as a configuration of the referring expressions 'this' and 'green' leads to an oversimplified conception of the way in which objects in the world are pictured by statements as complex natural-linguistic objects. This oversimplified conception (cf. Bergmann) is tied to a Platonic realism with respect to universals. For an elaboration of this point, see Chapter 7, SPR.

3=now

......

in the proper order one heartbeat apart, and continually inscribes statements of the form

/x,y,z/ = here

where the value of 'x' or 'y' or 'z' changes in a way illustrated by the sequence

/2,5,9/ = here      Step taken in direction $z_+$
/2,5,10/ = here.

These inscriptions, which give expression to the inscriber's awareness of where is here and when is now, are involved in uniformities of the following kind. The inscriber observes a green object immediately in front of him. He inscribes,

This here now is green      /2,5,9/ = here      4 = now

and proceeds to inscribe

... /2,5,9;4/ is green      /2,5,9/ = here      5 = now.

Roughly, he goes from a "this here now statement" to a statement in which the event in question is referred to by a coordinate name.

109. Let us now suppose that whenever a "this here now" statement has been thus transformed, the inscriber keeps on inscribing the result at all subsequent moments. His inscriptions are cumulative.

110. Another supposition: The inscriber writes his inscriptions in an order that corresponds to an ordering of the names that appear in them according to the values of the numerals of which they are composed. To simplify, let us suppose that his space has only one dimension, so that names have the form '/s;t/', and that the principle of order is that of inscribing all sentences involving a given value of 't' in the order of the values of 's', thus:

... /9,t/ is green        /10,t/ is blue

and only after all inscriptions involving that value of 't' have been inscribed does the inscription continue with inscriptions involving the next value of 't', thus:

... /101,10/ is red        /9,11/ is blue.

111.    If we add that the inscriber writes numerals without the use of definitional abbreviations, so that the names have the form,

/O'''', O''''···'/

we see that the inscriptions will reflect, in their multiplicity, the multiplicities of *heartbeats* and *steps* that separate the events which, speaking from without, we know to be referred to by the inscriptions.

112.    We have taken into account, so far, of some, at least, of the uniformities that reflect the conceptual processes involved in the observation and retention of matters of fact. The next step is to take into account the fact that our inscriber is, in the full sense, a rational being. For, in the rich inner life we have given him and which is only partially expressed by the inscriptions he makes, there is a substantial body of inductive knowledge. And without this inductive knowledge there can be no rational extension of one's picture of the world beyond what has been observed and retained. Let us imagine that, whatever the form of the reasoning by which one infers from the occurrence of an observed event of one kind to the occurrence of an unobserved event of another by means of an inductive generalization, it finds its expression at the inscriptional level in a sequence of two inscriptions, the former of which describes the observed event, while the latter describes the inferred event. And, as in the case of observation, let us suppose that once the latter inscription is inscribed, it continues to be inscribed.

113.    Before attempting to draw any morals from this story of an industrious super-inscriber, let me remind you that inscriptions of the form

/x,y,z;t/ is green

must not be construed as involving two names, '/x,y,z;t/' and 'green'. The whole inscription '/x,y,z;t/ is green' *is to be construed as a way* of writing the *one* name '/x,y,z;t/'. Again, more intuitively, given the above account of the arranging and rearranging of the elementary inscriptions, two names, by virtue of occurring in a certain order, constitute a dyadic relational statement to the effect that the objects named stand in a certain spatiotemporal relationship to one another.

114.   But, whatever subtleties might have to be added to the above to make it do its work, an objection can be raised to the whole enterprise. For, it might be argued, even if it were made to work, it could not do what I want it to do. For, surely, I have at best indicated how a structure of natural-linguistic objects might correspond, by virtue of certain "rules of projection" to a structure of nonlinguistic objects. But to say that a manifold of linguistic objects *correctly* pictures a manifold of nonlinguistic objects is no longer to consider them as mere "natural-linguistic objects"—to use your term—but to consider them as linguistic objects proper, and to say that they are *true*. Thus, instead of finding a mode of "correspondence" *other than truth* that accompanies truth in the case of empirical statements, your "correspondence" is simply truth all over again.

115.   So the objection. I reply that to say that a linguistic object *correctly* pictures a nonlinguistic object in the manner described above is not to say that the linguistic object is *true*, save in that metaphorical sense of 'true' in which one geometrical figure can be said to be a "true" projection of another if it is drawn by correctly following the appropriate method of projection.

116.   If it is objected that to speak of a linguistic structure as a *correct* projection is to use normative language and, therefore, to violate the terms of the problem which was to define 'picturing' as a relation in *rerum natura*, the answer is that, while to say of a projection that it is *correct* is, indeed, to use normative language, the principle which, it will be remembered, I am taking as axiomatic assures us that corresponding to every espoused principle of correctness there is a matter-of-factual uniformity in performance. And it is such uniformities, which link natural-linguistic objects with one another and with the objects of which they are the linguistic projections, that constitute picturing as a relation of matter of fact between objects in the natural order.

117.   And, indeed, it seems to me that, given the assumptions we have been making, the matter-of-factual uniformities exhibited by our ideal inscriber are the counterpart of "rules of projection" in terms of which an inscription string can be regarded as a projection of the spatiotemporal region in which the inscriber has

been moving around, observing and inferring.

[Editorial remark: material not included by Sellars]

[118.  We saw that, while *all* true statements of whatever kind are true in the same sense of 'true', the roles of different kinds of statement are different; thus the role of '2 plus 2 equals 4' is different from that of 'This is red'. My argument is that, in the case of matter-of-factual statements (and, in the last analysis, the acts of thought to which they give expression), this role is that of constituting a projection in language users of the world in which they live.

119.    Thus, while to say

That /9,7/ is green is true

is not to *say* that tokens of '/9,7/ is green' as natural-linguistic objects correspond in ways defined by certain rules of projection to the object /9,7/, and is, in an appropriate sense, its picture, yet it *implies* that it so corresponds. For to commit oneself to

That /9,7/ is green is true

is to commit oneself to

/9,7/ is green

and if to understand a language involves knowing (though not at the level of philosophical reflection) that uniformities such as were described in the myth of the perfect inscriber are involved in the use of language and if, therefore, I recognize (though not at the level of philosophical reflection) that, to the extent to which roles are executed and rules conformed to, statements are complex objects in a system that is a picture of natural events, surely I must recognize in my statement '/9,7/ is green' the projection of the object /9,7/.

120.    That the projection exists in any completeness at the level of *acts of thought* rather than statements is a theme the exploration of which would require a complete philosophy of mind.]

# CORRESPONDENCE WITH MICHAEL LOUX

June 23, 1978[1]

Professor Michael Loux
Department of Philosophy
University of Notre Dame
Notre Dame, Indiana 46556

Dear Mike:

1.      I have been reading the proofs of the Pitt book and pondering the many interesting questions raised and difficulties pointed out by my friends and critics. I have just been rereading your truly excellent essay on my theory of abstract entities. Since this theory is an essential part of the 'system', if it is radically mistaken, I would really be in trouble. Your essay cuts right to the heart of the matter and requires an answer. I must at least ward off some of the more telling blows sufficiently well to keep the theory alive and in readiness for the next stage of the argument. We shall see.

2.      To make things manageable, I shall limit myself to the theory proper. Thus I shall postpone to another occasion such topics as quantification theory and the analysis of real numbers. These are complex problems in their own right which must be dealt with by any theory of abstract entities, though it may well be that my theory is particularly sensitive to them. Furthermore, I shall not take up the questions in the order in which you raise them. After all, your purpose is as much to explain the theory as to evaluate it, so that you often raise difficulties in order to answer them yourself, and by so doing exhibit its power and complexity. It is only when you reach the stage of finding difficulties but no answers that I must intervene.

3.      This stage is reached on page 244 where you write:

---

[1] This letter is a reply to Loux's "Rules, Roles, and Ontological Commitment: an Examination of Sellars' Analysis of Abstract Reference," in Joseph C. Pitt (ed.) *The Philosophy of Wilfrid Sellars: Queries and Extensions*, Dordrecht-Holland, 1978.

> Abstract singular terms may represent the paradigmatic vehicles of abstract singular reference, but they do not exhaust our linguistic resources for "referring" to the so-called abstract entities. Definite descriptions also function as what appear to be abstract singular referring devices, and no nominalistic theory can claim to be satisfactory unless it has the resources for providing an account of sentences where the apparent vehicle of abstract reference is a definite description.

This is certainly true, and it serves to introduce the problem with which the concluding and more critical sections of your essay are concerned. It is interesting to note, however, that even after introducing this general theme, you find yourself able to find resources in the theory for constructing plausible answers to the initial difficulties it generates.

4.     You begin with the problem of transcribing into the language of the theory

(11)    The color exemplified by Amy Carter's ball is a property.

You are led to propose first,

(11-b) The color-predicate which is truly predicable of Amy Carter's ball is an adjective

and then, more formally,

(11-c) $(\exists \text{PRECON}_i)[(\text{PRECON}_j)(\text{PRECON}_j = \text{PRECON}_i . \equiv . \text{PRECON}_j$ is a color predicate truly predicable of Amy Carter's ball) and $\text{PRECON}_i$ is an adjective].

Although some features of (11-c) are clearly problematic, the above sequence shows that the theory can make at least a plausible beginning at giving an account of sentences which refer to abstract entities by the use of definite descriptions. However, a different example leads to difficulties which, in the long run, you find insuperable. Some of the difficulties fall in the category which, as indicated above, I shall postpone until a later occasion. Others, however, are specific to the theory, and I turn immediately to the task of coping with them. The example, presented on the bottom of page 247, is the following:

(13)   The attribute most frequently ascribed to Alcibiades is a property.

You begin your discussion of this example by pointing out that if, as suggested by the Amy Carter example, we begin by construing (13) as equivalent to

(13-a) The predicate-term most frequently predicated of Alcibiades is an adjective,

we run into the fact that

> Although the most common way of ascribing treachery to Alcibiades is to predicate a 'treacherous' of him, there are other ways. We can say, for example, that he exemplifies the attribute the Athenians found most abhorrent. But, then, it could turn out that while treachery is the attribute most frequently ascribed to Alcibiades, some other predicate-term (say a common noun like 'soldier') has been predicated of him with greater frequency...so that it is possible for (13) to be...true and for (13-b) ...to turn out false

where (13-b) is

(13-b) ($\exists$ $PC_i$)[($PC_j$)$PC_j$ = $PC_i$ $.\equiv.$ $PC_j$ is a predicate-term predicated of Alcibiades more frequently than any other predicate-term) and $PC_i$ is an adjective]

which is (13-a) "in more formal garb."

5.     But *is* the theory committed to (13-a) as the reconstruction of (13)? Only if ascribing an attribute is construed as predicating the predicate-term which stands to the attribute as does 'triangular' to triangularity, or being triangular. But, clearly, for the reasons you give in the passage quoted above, one can ascribe triangularity to an object without using a •triangular• and treachery to Alcibiades without using a •treacherous•. It follows that to make the strategy work it would have to be possible to predicate •treacherous• of Alcibiades without using a •treacherous•. Does this make sense? I suggest that it does and that the desired result can be achieved by distinguishing between two ways in which a predicate-term can be said to be predicated of an object. Let me distinguish these two ways as, respectively, "direct" and "indirect." This I do, schematically, as follows, where

't' is a variable ranging over expression-tokens, '∈' represents 'is a' and '⌒' represents concatenation:

PC$_i$ is predicated of O iff

    (1)   (∃t) t ∈ PC$_i$⌒•O•                       [direct]

or

    (2)   PC$_i$ is the PC such that PC is φ and

           (∃t) t ∈ •the PC such PC is φ is true of O•    [indirect]

Since it begs no question at issue, the reference to the object is taken to be by name, 'O' representing the name and '•O•' its dot-quoted counterpart. The relevant example which satisfies this scheme would be

•Treacherous• is predicated of Alcibiades iff

    (1)   (∃t) t ∈ •treacherous•⌒•Alcibiades•

or

    (2)   •Treacherous• is the PC such that PC is φ and (∃t) t ∈ •the PC such that PC is φ is true of Alcibiades•.

Disjunct (1) tells us that there is a token of

•treacherous•⌒•Alcibiades•.

I generate the following token, t$_1$, thus

Treacherous Alcibiades [Alcibiades is treacherous].

The first line of disjunct (2) tells us that •treacherous• is the predicate term which uniquely satisfies condition φ (left for the moment in schematic form). The second line of (2) tells us that there is a token of •The PC such that PC is φ is true of Alcibiades•. I generate the following token, t$_2$, thus

The PC such that PC is φ is true of Alcibiades.

The former token, t$_1$, directly predicates •treacherous• of Alcibiades; the second, t$_2$, does so "indirectly."

6.    Given this distinction, thus explicated, we can offer the following reconstruction of (13):

(13-c) There are more tokens which either directly or indirectly predicate •treacherous• of Alcibiades than there are which directly or indirectly predicate any other PC of Alcibiades.

7.    Now while the possibility of the above strategy does not seem to have occurred to you, you make a not unrelated move. Whereas I have proposed a disjunctive analysis of 'PC is predicated of x' you consider the possibility of a disjunctive analysis of 'x is a property', thus

x is a property $=_{df}$
either    (a) •y•s are adjectives (where 'x' is an abstract singular term and 'y' its
         concrete counterpart)
or       (b) for some z, x is identical with z and z is a property in the sense of (a).

Your reaction to this definition is complex. You begin by calling attention to the use of the phrase 'is identical with' in clause (b), and by challenging the theory to come up with a satisfactory account of the relevant sense of sameness or identity. You ask, in effect: What is to be the reconstructed counterpart of the 'is' of

(15)    The attribute most frequently ascribed to Alcibiades *is* treachery?

This question has clearly been hovering in the wings and it is high time that it came to front and center stage. But instead of pressing this challenge, you begin by reformulating your previous objection to (13-b) so that it applies to what you suppose the theory will offer as a reconstruction of (15), i.e.,

(15-a) The predicate-term most frequently predicated of Alcibiades is •treacherous•.

You let the 'is' slip in unheralded—for the moment, at least—and argue that (15-a) won't do as a reconstruction of (15) because, while (15) is true, (15-a) could be false. But if my disjunctive analysis of 'PC is predicated of x' is on the right track, the argument fails, and we are back where we were—with the (important) exception that the challenge which preceded the argument remains to be dealt with.

8.       How, indeed, are statements of attribute identities to be analyzed? "What is needed," you point out, "is a general account of sentences which appear to ascribe identity to abstract entities." (p. 251). At this point you embark on a wild goose chase, motivated by the hypothesis that the only strategy open to me is that of invoking the "Sellarsian notion of material equivalence." My off-the-cuff remarks at Blacksburg undoubtedly played a part in reinforcing this hypothesis. My thinking-out-loud in an attempt to grasp the exact force of your Alcibiades example (with which I had just been confronted) was not particularly successful, and certainly misleading. However that may be, you are quite right to argue that material equivalence will not do the job. Yet the suggestion is not entirely without merit, for a superficially similar strategy does work. It will be worthwhile, therefore, to examine the situation at some length, for this will lay the groundwork for the correct solution.

9.       Material equivalence is the semantical concept which corresponds to the truth functional connective ' $\equiv$ ' in the object language. Thus

•Socrates• ME •the teacher of Plato•

which has the sense of

$(PC)(PC^\frown\bullet Socrates\bullet$ is true $\equiv PC^\frown\bullet$the teacher of Plato• is true$)^2$

corresponds to

Socrates = the teacher of Plato

where the latter, in accordance with the Leibnitz-Russell definition of the identity of individuals, is to be construed as

---

[2] This is equivalent to

$(PC)(PC$ is true of Socrates $\equiv PC$ is true of the teacher of Plato$)$.

But to spell out this equivalence would require a discussion at length of the context 'true of'. The discussion would make clear (*vide* your remarks on p. 252) that '•Socrates• ME •the teacher of Plato•' can be the semantical counterpart of 'Socrates = the teacher of Plato' only if Socrates denotes Socrates and hence has a denotation.

(f) f(Socrates) ≡ f(the teacher of Plato).

I have pointed out in a number of places, most recently in my "Reply to Quine" (EPH, p. 171, fn. 16) that it would philosophically more perspicuous to write

Socrates ≡ the teacher of Plato

for this would emphasize that the identity in question is no more to be construed as a relational *predicate* than the truth functional connective ('≡') in terms of which it is defined.

10. Again

(2) •featherless biped• ME •rational animal•

has in first approximation the sense of

(x) •featherless biped• is true of x ≡ •rational animal• is true of x

and, hence, corresponds to

(2-a) featherless biped = rational animal

where this is construed as definitionally equivalent to

(2-b) (x) x is a featherless biped ≡ x is a rational animal.

Here it would be philosophically perspicuous to write (2-a) as

(2-c) featherless biped ≡ rational animal

to emphasize the predicative character of the expressions 'featherless biped' and 'rational animal' as they occur in a context which is definitionally equivalent to (2-b). *Thus construed*, (2-a) is to be carefully distinguished from

(2-d) FB = RA

where the expressions which flank the identity sign are functioning as "names" of classes. The latter are a variety of abstract entities and as such require a Sellarsian treatment. Indeed, (2-d), thus construed, belongs to the semantical meta-language and has in first approximation the sense of (2).

11.    It is crucial, therefore, not to confuse (2) with either its object language counterparts—(2-a), (2-b) and (2-c)—or with its meta-linguistic *cousin*

(3)     •featherless biped• ≡ •rational animal•

which is, of course, false since it says that something is a (token of) •featherless biped• if and only if it is a (token of) •rational animal•, i.e.,

(3-a)   (x) x is a •featherless biped• ≡ x is a •rational animal•.

12.    In putting the concept of material equivalence to work in connection with the problem at hand, you suggest that we look for a statement of the form

•treachery• ME ... .

And, indeed, at first sight this seems to be the natural move to make, since the task is to reconstruct

Treachery *is* ...[3].

---

[3]Yet that something has gone wrong is suggested by the fact that

•Socrates• ME •the teacher of Plato•

does *not* reconstruct (though it is logically equivalent to)

Socrates *is* the teacher of Plato

any more than

•Snow is white• is true

*reconstructs*

Snow is white.

You offer

(15-b) •treachery• ME •the attribute most frequently ascribed to Alcibiades•.

According to the analysis of '•Socrates• ME •the teacher of Plato•' (given above), this would tell us (using 'the A-attribute' to abbreviate 'the attribute most frequently ascribed to Alcibiades') that

(PC)(PC⁀•treachery• is true ≡ PC⁀•the A-attribute• is true)

which would be the higher level counterpart of

(f)f(treachery) ≡ f(the A-attribute)

and, hence, of

treachery = A-attribute.

This, however, does not advance our problem, for while it tells us, correctly, that (15-b) is true if and only if treachery is the A-attribute, it requires that (15-b) be on a semantical level one step higher than (15), the statement we are trying to reconstruct. It also, as you point out, requires that the 'treachery' of (15) have a different sense than 'treachery' as it occurs in

(17)   Quine abhors treachery

and, most damagingly, as it occurs in

(18)   Treachery is a property.

You pull these latter considerations together by pointing out that '(15), (17) and (18) taken conjunctively, entail

(19)   A property Quine abhors is the attribute most frequently ascribed to Alcibiades

and the entailment would seem to presuppose that 'treachery' is a single expression in each of (15), (17) and (18)." (p. 252).

13.    Now all of this obviously suggests (as hinted in footnote 3 above) that if the concept of material equivalence is to help it should be applied one level down. Thus, instead of looking at statements beginning

•treachery• ME ...

which, as you point out, becomes, when parsed according to the theory, the double dot-quoted

•The •treacherous•• ME ...,

the higher level status of which is explicit, we should, perhaps, try

•Treacherous• ME... .

What about

(15-d) •Treacherous• ME the PC such that PC is most frequently predicated of A?

If we follow the principle of the account given above of '•featherless biped• ME •rational animal•', (15-d) would tell us that

(x) •treacherous• is true of x ≡ the PC such that PC is most frequently predicated of Alcibiades is true of x.

This is true, and at first glance it solves our problem. It is, however, open to a devastating objection. For suppose it to be true that

(x) x is treacherous ≡ x is a psychopath.

Then it would also be true that

(x) •treacherous• is true of x ≡ •psychopath• is true of x

and hence that

(x) •psychopath• is true of x ≡ the PC such that PC is most frequently predicated of Alcibiades is true of x

which, according to the proposed analysis, would entail that

The attribute most frequently ascribed to Alcibiades is being a psychopath

which is false.

14.    We clearly need a stronger relation than that of a material equivalence
between dot-quoted sortals. On the other hand, it is a mistake to move as quickly
as you do to the idea that the fault lies in working with extensional contexts. You
write, "The difficulty, of course, is that material equivalence is an extensional
notion and, consequently, is too weak to serve as an explication of the concept of
identity as it applies to attributes." (p. 253). For it is an *essential* part of the
Sellarsian strategy to treat intensional contexts as material mode counterparts of
meta-linguistic extensional contexts. The problems of intensional entities and
intensional contexts are as inseparable as Quine finds them to be. A Sellarsian
"nominalist" must be a Sellarsian "extensionalist." (It will turn out, however, that
a Sellarsian "extensionalist" in statement-logic preserves the core of the "extensional"-"intensional" dualism by tracing it to a contrast of quite a different kind.)
15.    You write

> Why is it that •Socrates•s are co-extensional with •the teacher of Plato•s and why is
> it that •the •treacherous•s are co-extensional with •the attribute most frequently ascribed
> to Alcibiades•s? Precisely because Socrates *was* the teacher of Plato and treachery *is* the
> attribute most frequently ascribed to Alcibiades. Talk of defining identity away, then, by
> means of the metalinguistic expedient of material equivalence, however reinforced, is
> wrong-headed; it puts the •cart• before the horse. (p. 253).

This challenge, neatly put, lays the cards on the table. But it also reveals a basic
misunderstanding. I do *not* "define identity away" by means of material equivalence. That would be a confusion of semantic levels. I simply accept the Leibnitz-

Russell definition of the identity of individuals in terms of predicate quantification and the connective 'if and only if'. The statement

•Socrates• ME •the teacher of Plato•

is logically equivalent to *but not synonymous with*

Socrates = the teacher of Plato.

The latter is an object language extensional context and has the sense of

(f)f(Socrates) ≡ f(the teacher of Plato).

16.    Can we limit ourselves to extensional contexts and yet find a stronger relation between metalinguistic sortals than material equivalence? The initial clue to the answer lies in the difference between

(24)    •f• ME •g•
and
(25)    •f• ≡ •g•

where the later contrived expression has the form

(26)    $K_1 \equiv K_2$

where this is equivalent by definition to

(27)    (x) x is a $K_1$ ≡ x is a $K_2$.

Notice that according to this explication, (25) tells us that everything which is a token of •f• is a token of •g• and vice versa. Is this the stronger relation between predicate constants for which we are looking in our search for the relevant sameness? Well, it is clearly stronger than material equivalence, but will it do the job?
17.    What about

(15-e) •treacherous• ≡ the PC such that PC is most frequently predicated of

Alcibiades

as a reconstruction of (15)? Can we not replace the '$\equiv$' by '=' (i.e., 'is the same as') as we did in the case of

Socrates $\equiv$ the teacher of Plato?

We would then have as our analysis of (15)

(15-f) The •treacherous• = the PC such that PC is most frequently predicated of A.

Unfortunately, once again there is an obvious objection. It begins by reminding us that predicates which are true of nothing are coextensive. Thus

centaur $\equiv$ dragon.

By parity of reasoning, if •f•and •g• are untokened, then

(25)    •f• $\equiv$ •g•

whatever •f• and •g• may be. Hence, if the identity of the attributes f-ness and g-ness is equated with (25) we would be forced to say that two attributes which have never been expressed by tokens, as triangularity (being triangular) is expressed by tokens of •triangular•, would be the "same." (Notice that this is quite different from saying that any two unexemplified attributes would be the same).

18.    The objection can be pressed home as follows. Let 's' be the variable for which dot-quoted expressions are substituted. Can we say that

(28)    $s_i$ is the same as $s_j$ .$\equiv$. $s_i \equiv s_j$?

If, as I have done, we call 's' the variable for senses, would we not have to say that all untokened senses are the same? It would seem that

$s_i \equiv s_j$

can at best be a necessary but not a sufficient condition for

$$s_i = s_j.$$

19.    It will be helpful to consider a related problem which is faced by the theory. That-clauses, it tells us, are to be reconstructed as distributive singular terms formed from dot-quoted sentences. Thus,

that fa

is reconstructed as

the •fa•.

Now we consider the following argument:

1. that fa is true ≡ the •fa• is true                   Expl. 'that'
2. The •fa• is true ≡ •fa•s are true                   DST
3. •fa•s are true ≡ (t)t ∈ •fa• ⊃ t is true             Formalization
4. (t)t ∈ •fa• ⊃ t is true ≡ ~(∃t)t ∈ •fa• & ~(t is true)   Theorem
5. ~(∃t)t ∈ •fa• ⊃ ~(∃t)t ∈ •fa• & ~(t is true)        Theorem
6. ~(∃t)t ∈ •fa•                                        Hyp.
7. ~(∃t)t ∈ •fa• & ~(t is true)                         5, 6, MP
8. (t)t ∈ •fa• ⊃ t is true                              7, logic
9. That fa is true                                      8, 3, 2, 1

Since the argument holds quite generally and since the operative premise is 6, which says that •fa• has no tokens, we have ostensibly established the principle that

(Π)    ~(∃t) t ∈ Π ⊃ Π is true

where 'Π' is the variable for propositional senses.

20.    Notice, however, that if the predicate 'true' is reconstructed as 'semantically assertible', as according to the theory it should be, the argument fails. For if 'assertible' has the sense of '*may* be asserted', there is hanky-panky in premise

3. The point stands out clearly if we consider the following argument schema, where φ represents an arbitrary predicate.

| | |
|---|---|
| 1. Trespassers are φ ≡ (x)x ∈ T ⊃ φx | Formalization |
| 2. (x)x ∈ T ⊃ φx ≡ ~(∃x)(x ∈ T & ~φx) | Theorem |
| 3. ~(∃x)x ∈ T ⊃ ~(∃x)(x ∈ T & ~φx) | Theorem |
| 4. ~(∃x)x ∈ T | Hyp. |
| 5. ~(∃x)(x ∈ T & ~φx) | 3, 4, MP |
| 6. (x)x ∈ T ⊃ φx | 2, 5, MP |
| 7. Trespassers are φ | 1, 6 |

Here again the argument is quite general, this time explicitly so. Therefore, given that there are no trespassers, we are ostensibly entitled to conclude that

(φ) Trespassers are φ

for example,

Trespassers are bald
Trespassers are longhaired.

But what of

Trespassers are praiseworthy?
Trespassers are blameworthy?

or, to come to the heart of the matter,

Trespassers are prosecutable
i. e.,
Trespassers *may* be prosecuted?

a cousin of an old (and much neglected) friend. It is obviously incorrect to take step 2 above as a (schematic) representation of the logical powers of

Trespassers are prosecutable.

A perspicuous transcription of the latter would not be

(x) x ∈ T ⊃ x is prosecutable

but rather—at least in first approximation—

Permitted ((x) x ∈ T ⊃ x is prosecuted)

which neither entails nor is entailed by

~(∃x)x ∈ T.

By parity of reasoning '•fa•s are semantically assertible' neither entails nor is entailed by '~(Et)t ∈ •fa•' and the principle

(Π)     ~(∃t) t ∈ Π ⊃ Π is true

fails.

21.     Clearly the key to the above reasoning is the distinction between 'declarative' and 'prescriptive' contexts. The latter are grounded in rules. This is why

f-ness = g-ness

is stronger than

•f• ≡ •g•

for it tells us not only that all tokens of •f• are tokens of •g• (and vice versa), but in the very process of doing so tells us that all inscriptions which *conform* to the rules for •f•s also conform to the rules for •g•s (and vice versa). Nothing which did not so conform would count as a token (in a primary sense) of either •f• or •g•. And it is the rules which guarantee that were anything to be a token of •f• it *would* be a token of •g•.

22.     In footnote 30 you write, "Sellars wants to claim that we can specify identity-conditions for attributes by reference to linguistic rules. Thus F-ness = G-

ness is true just in case •F•s and •G•s are subject to precisely the same linguistic rules." You object that "This account of the identity-conditions works only for sentences in which we employ abstract singular terms as our device for picking out attributes." By 'works' you seem to mean 'can be effectively applied to determine particular identities'. It is of course true that I can determine that two attributes are identical only if I know the rules for the relevant predicate constants and can show that they are the same. But this by no means entails that a general reference to sameness of rules cannot explicate the concept of attribute identity. I can surely refer to rules which I do not have up my sleeves. Thus I can say that for all $s_i$ and $s_j$,

$$s_i = s_j$$

if and only if $s_i$ and $s_j$ are roles which occupy the same place in a system of roles specified by a set of rules. Of course, in the case of

rapidity = quickness,

i.e.,

The •rapid• = the •quick•,

I can actually work out the relevant rules by rehearsing our use of •rapid• and •quick•, which, of course, I cannot do for unspecified $s_i$ and $s_j$.

23.    Two asides. In the first place your remarks (pp. 240-1) on Wolterstorff's criticism of my concept of distributive singular terms is exactly to the point. Whenever I have run into this criticism, I have taken the same line, which was foreshadowed in my original account in "Abstract Entities." In the second place, I was puzzled by your puzzlement on p. 242, where you comment on my "admission" that I "countenance such exotic abstract entities as functions, roles, rules and pieces." But surely all I am saying in the passage you quote is that abstract singular terms for these entities are to be handled by the same strategy as is used to handle 'triangularity'. As for the specific nature of abstract entities belonging to these categories, the lines I take is, essentially, the one you hit upon on p. 243. What else could I do?

24.    It is time that I concluded this lengthy essay on your essay, not because I have laid to rest all the questions you raise—I haven't—but because to say more I would have to say a great deal more and, perhaps, more than I now know how to

say. Let me express, however, the hope that what I have said has cleared away some sources of misunderstanding and, perhaps, prepared the way for a further exchange of views which might take us closer to the exit from the Labyrinth. The problem of abstract entities is so many problems in one, that to resolve it a complete metaphysics would be necessary. A letter is no place for that. I have already dodged ("postponed") some of the larger issues you have raised. Perhaps there are still some smaller, but strategic, difficulties which stand in the way of the theory. Indeed, perhaps the argument of this letter is flawed in ways I have not noticed. Anything you have to say would be welcome.

Cordially,
Wilfrid Sellars

October 6, 1978

Professor Wilfrid Sellars
Department of Philosophy
University of Pittsburgh
Pittsburgh, PA 15260

Dear Wilfrid:

25.    Your letter is extremely helpful in clarifying a number of issues. At first, I had trouble with your distinction between direct and indirect predication. I just couldn't fasten on the appropriate substituends for the variables in the formulae in paragraph 5; but after some reflection, I came to see the force of the distinction; and I agree that it is a metalinguistic cousin of my disjunctive analysis of being a property. I also agree that if either account could be supplemented with a general account of sentences expressing attribute-identity (including those where the '=' is flanked by definite descriptions), then you'd have a satisfactory response to the difficulties my counterexamples raise. I further agree with the basic thrust of paragraphs 7-17.

26.    Before I get to what I take to be your final account of the relevant identity-sentences, let me clarify one point. I had not meant to attribute to you the view that sentences of the form '•x• ME •y•' define sentences of the form 'x = y'. As my last footnote indicates, I as suggesting a move that the defender of the Sellarsian treatment of abstract terms (but obviously not the Sellars of *Science and*

*Metaphysics*) might invoke to get out of my difficulties with (15).

27.    The account you want to suggest is formalized in paragraph 17 in (15-e); at least that's how I read your remarks. I have a couple of problems with (15-e). The first is perhaps just a small problem; and clarification on your part will probably dispel it. The difficulty is that I don't see how to read the reconstruction of (15-e), which would have the form

(x)(x is a •treacherous• ≡ ....).

28.    What I'm not sure about is the right hand side of the bi-conditional. How are we to read that? Clearly the substituends for 'x' have to be names of tokens of •treacherous•; but then we can't read the right hand side of the biconditional as 'x is the PC such that ...', for no token is the predicate constant most frequently ascribed to Alcibiades; but neither can we say 'x is a token of the PC ...', because then we're stuck with a type-token distinction that the strategy of DSTs won't (at least not obviously) be able to eliminate.

29.    My second problem with (15-e) and, in general, the strategy for handling attribute-identity outlined in paragraphs 18-22 bears on the problem you so lucidly identify, that of untokened linguistic types. You try to handle the difficulty by appeal to an analogy. I think I see how the analogy works. At least, I think I see the point about the prescriptive force of 'true', and I think I understand how you want to apply the moral about 'true' to the case of dot quotation generally. The idea (expressed in paragraph 22) is that dot quotation involves us in talk about rules, norms, conformity, etc., so that there is a kind of subjunctive or modal flavor implicit in claims of the form

•g• ≡ •f•;

and you want to suggest that the result is that untokened linguistic types don't all come out identical on your account.

30.    Now, it may just be a blind-spot on my part; but I don't see how the relevant normative flavor of dot quotation has the consequence you claim for it. Even though being an •f• and being a •g• do involve rule-conformities, isn't it still the case that, where we have two untokened linguistic types, everything is such that it is a token of one iff it is a token of the other? Or, to put it in another way, isn't it still true that there is nothing for which it is not true that it is a token of the one

type iff it is a token of the other? The universal quantifier and the biconditional are as extensional here as they are anywhere else, and as I see it, that's all that's required to generate the result you want to avoid.

31.     Perhaps, an example (it may not be very appropriate, but here goes anyway) will help. Suppose we have a pair of distinct actions, A and $A^1$, that no one has ever performed. Perhaps, the social sanctions against A and $A^1$ are both strong and successful. Now the concepts of *being an A* and *being an $A^1$* are as rule-involving as one could want; to perform A, one *must* ... and to perform $A^1$, one *must* ...; but despite the rule-conformity involved here, the supposition that there are no instances of A or $A^1$ has the effect, I think, that

$$(x)(\text{is an instance of } A \equiv x \text{ is an instance of } A^1)$$

is true. As I see it, the prescriptivity ingredient in our notions of A and $A^1$ just doesn't alter the through-and-through extensionality of the universal biconditional.

32.     Of course, one could avoid the problem with untokened types by modalizing •g• $\equiv$ •f•, so that it is to be understood as

$$\text{Necessarily, } (x)(x \text{ is a •g•} \equiv x \text{ is an •f•});$$

but obviously a philosopher like yourself, who wants to explain modality in terms of the rules of language, wouldn't want to make that alteration in the account.

33.     Another possible move here is to take •f• $\equiv$ •g• to involve quantification with respect to tokenings of an omniscient language-user; but, to invoke the language of omniscience here, I think you'd have to confront the other difficulties I point to in my discussion of your theory of quantification.

34.     Anyway, those are my problems. They're probably due to misunderstanding; but even if they are, I'd be interested in your reflections on my reflections on your ... . It is, after all, an old debate; and if you can't convince me, then we can argue about something else—whether we are ideal inquirers or whether the Peircian definition of truth is true!

Sincerely

Michael J. Loux

November 6, 1978

Professor Michael Loux
Department of Philosophy
University of Notre Dame
Notre Dame, Indiana 46556

Dear Mike:

35.    Thanks for the quick reply to my letter. It advances the discussion apace.

36.    First your query about how to read (15-e). This is the easy one. You were misled by its surface grammar, and failed to take into account the fact that 'the PC such that PC is *a*' is functioning as a quantified *predicative* expression. Your platonistic eye for singular terms is the source of your trouble. It led you to the construction

(x)x *is a* •treacherous• ≡ x *is* the PC such that ...

where the 'is' on the right hand side is parsed as the 'is' of identity. The result, as you note, is incoherent. The truth of the matter is that what is needed is the 'is a' of sortal predication—in other words my '$\epsilon_1$' as contrasted with the '$\epsilon_2$' of set membership.[1]

37.    Let me contrive a simpler example which raises the same problem of interpretation. Consider

(1)    Man ≡ a sort such that that sort is an animal.[2]

How do we read this, when we make explicit the quantification over individuals which it involves? The left hand side poses no problem

(x) x is a man ≡ ...

What about the right hand side? One might be tempted to try

---

[1] Since I am not concerned with this contrast in this letter, I shall represent 'is a' by '$\epsilon$'.

[2] The basic statement form with which I am concerned is illustrated by 'The cow is an animal' which is the distributive singular term version of 'cows are animals'.

≡ x *is* a sort such that ... .

But this would be a mistake; indeed, the very one you made. To get on the right track we must first take seriously the idea that if there is to be a coherent reading, the right hand side must also have the form

x *is a* [sortal predicate].

Furthermore we must bear in mind that the phrase 'a sort' on the right hand side of (1) is a quantified predicate variable and is to be represented symbolically by '(∃s)', i.e., 'for some s', where 's' is a variable which takes sortals for substituends. These requirements are met by

(∃s) s ⊂ animal & x is an s

which we might try to put in English as

For some sort which is an animal, x is an *it*.

From this vantage point, we can see that the desired symbolic representation of (1) is

(1-a)   (∃s) s ⊂ animal & (x) x ∈ man ≡ x ∈ s.

38.     Armed with hindsight we can now see that if we had tried to move directly from the right hand side of (1) to its underlying logical form by introducing 'x is a ...' we would have run the danger of confusing the 'a' of 'is a' with the 'a' of 'a sort'. To avoid this, we would have had to have written

x is a(n) a sort such that ... .

The mistake to which I called attention consists exactly in eliding the 'a' of 'is a' with the 'a' of 'a sort'.

39.     All that remains to be done is to apply these considerations to (15-e). If we do, we get

(15e-1)   (∃ PC) PC is most frequently predicated of Alcibiades & (x) x ∈ •treacherous• ≡ x ∈ PC.[3]

40.   Now for the more difficult challenge. You write

> ... I don't see how the relevant normative flavor of dot quotation has the consequence you claim for it. Even though being an •f• and being a •g• do involve rule conformities, isn't it still the case that, where we do have two untokened linguistic types, everything is such that it is a token of one iff it is a token of the other?

The answer, clearly, is Yes! But your query makes manifest an *ignoratio elenchi*. My argument was designed to show *not* that if the predicates 'φ' and 'ψ' have a "normative flavor" then, to use your words, this "alter[s] the through and through extentionality of the biconditional"

(x) x is a φ ≡ x is a ψ

strengthening it so that its truth would not follow from the fact that φ and ψ are empty. It was rather, and you can check with paragraphs 20-22 of my letter, that it is a mistake to think that

Trespassers are prosecutable

has, other than superficially, the form

(x) x is a T ⊃ x is prosecutable.

I argued that, in first approximation, it has the deeper form

Permitted [(x) x is a T ⊃ x is prosecuted]

---

[3] Strictly speaking, to capture the definite description flavor of this particular example, we should be able to introduce a quantifier which is the second-order counterpart of the first order quantifier '∃!x'—'for some unique x'. But to introduce it is not necessary for the point I am now making and would, furthermore, raise all the questions about the *sameness* of predicate constants which I am concerned with in this letter.

which, I pointed out, neither entails nor is entailed by

~(∃x) x is a T.

I wrote "in first approximation" because to develop the point beyond the intuitive level I would have had to elaborate my theory of practical reasoning and, in particular, of the 'shall' operator.

41.     I now see that I will have to say something along those lines. Consider the sentences

(1) All trespassers are prosecuted.
(2) Let all trespassers be prosecuted!
(3) All trespassers ought to be prosecuted.

How are these related? I shall answer this question in terms of something like Hare's theory of imperative discourse. (1) has the form 'all As are Bs' and can be represented for our purposes as

(1a) (x) x is a T ⊃ x is prosecuted.

On the other hand, (2) has the form

(2a)    Let [(x) x is a T ⊃ x be prosecuted]!

where the brackets indicate the scope of the imperative operator, while (3) has the form

(3a)    'Let [(x) x is a T ⊃ x be prosecuted]!' is valid,

where 'valid' has the intuitive meaning 'is binding with respect to a relevant class of persons', which I will not attempt to analyze. I shall assume that the relevant class of persons is *we*.

42.     Given this framework, we can say that—and again I speak intuitively—(3a) entails (2a). Furthermore (1a) neither entails nor is entailed by either (2a) or (3a).

43.     Consider, now, a game which will never by played—let us suppose it to be chess. And let us introduce the terms 'pawn' and 'bishop' as short, respectively,

for 'object which has made or will make pawn-maneuvers' and 'object which has made or will make bishop-maneuvers'. We clearly want to be able to say both

The pawn is not the same as the bishop

and

(x) x is a pawn $\equiv$ x is a bishop.

The latter, given the above stipulations, is true.

44.    Now a Leibnitz-type principle tells us that

(L)    The $K_i$ is the same as the $K_j$ $\equiv$ every context which is true of the $K_i$ is true of the $K_j$.

If we apply this principle to a case of empty classes, we would get, for example,

The dragon is the same as the centaur.

For if a context of the form

All ... are $\varphi$

is true when '...' is replaced by 'dragons', it would also be true when '...' is replaced by 'centaurs'.

45.    At this point someone might be moved to expostulate, "Surely, an extensional logician can also take into account the extensions not only of the terms 'dragon' and 'centaur', but also of the Sellarsian terms '•dragon•' and '•centaur•', i.e., of 'dragonkind' and 'centaur-kind' construed as meta-linguistic sortals." "Obviously," they might continue, in a Goodmanian spirit, "the extensions of the latter terms are not null. If we call the extensions of '•dragon•' and '•centaur•' the *secondary* extensions of 'dragon' and 'centaur', respectively, might we not require that

The dragon is the same as the centaur

is true if and only if the primary *and the secondary* extensions of 'dragon' and 'centaur' coincide? Since the secondary extensions do not coincide—for there are inscriptions which are •dragon•s but not •centaur•s and *vice versa*—the above statement would be false."

46.    Very well and good. But suppose there were no tokens of these metalinguistic sortals: no •dragon•s nor •centaur•s. Would our extensionalist have to commit himself to the schema

$$K_i \text{ is the same as } K_j \; . \equiv . \; K_i \equiv K_j \text{ and } \dagger K_i \dagger \equiv \dagger K_j \dagger$$

where the dagger-quoted expressions represent the results of dot-quoting the substituends for 'K$_i$' and 'K$_j$'?

47.    This brings me back to the question pressed in paragraph 18 of my previous letter, which I quote:

> Let 's' be the variable for which dot-quoted expressions are substituted. Can we say that
>
> (28)    $s_i$ is the same as $s_j \; . \equiv . \; s_i \equiv s_j$?

which introduced the topic of untokened types.

48.    Now, we have already seen that the Leibnitz-like principle (L) does not give us what we want, even when reinforced by an appeal to secondary extensions. Is there any way in which, while remaining good extensionalists, we can get out of this jam?

49.    Consider the following generalization of (L):

(L′)    The K$_i$ is the same as the K$_j$ ≡ every context which *holds of* K$_i$ *holds of* K$_j$

where the key move is the substitution of 'holds of' for 'true of', the latter being a special case of the former. With this new principle, let us return to the chess example. The position was as follows. If we relied on (L) we were committed to

The pawn is the same as the bishop.

If we brought in secondary extensions, this helped with the pawn-bishop example, as it did with the dragon-centaur example, but beside its having an air of *ad-*

*hocery*, it left us with the general problem of the sameness of untokened types.
50. Does our new principle (L′) help? The answer is that it does. Let us go back
to our trespassers example, and consider

(3a) 'Let [(x) x is a trespasser ⊃ x be prosecuted]!' is valid.

We introduce the expression 'holds of' in such a way that

(4) 'Let [(x) x is a --- ⊃ x be prosecuted]!' holds of trespassers

is logically equivalent to (3a); and, in general, that

(5) 'Let [(x) x is a K ⊃ x be φ'd]!' is valid

is logically equivalent to

(6) 'Let [(x) x is a --- ⊃ x be φ'd]!' holds of Ks.

We now apply (L′) to our chess example as follows: Let '$M_p$' represent the
conjunction of admissible pawn-maneuvers, each conjunct specifying the conditions under which certain moves are permitted. And let '$M_b$' represent the
corresponding conjunction of admissible bishop-maneuvers. Then, although
according to (L)

The pawn is the same as the bishop

there being no pawns nor bishops, (L′) tells us that the pawn is not the same as the
bishop, since

'Let [(x) x is a --- ⊃ x be $M_p$'d]!' holds of pawns but not of bishops

while

'Let [(x) x is a --- ⊃ x be $M_b$'d]!' holds of bishops but not of pawns.

Notice that if we so construe 'rule' that a rule-like expression is a general imperative of the form

Let [(x) x is a $K_i \supset x$ be $M_i$'d]!

and a rule, an expression of this kind which is valid, we can introduce the term rule-matrix in such a way that

Let [(x)x is a --- $\supset x$ be $M_i$'d]!

is a rule-matrix which holds, for example, of $K_i$s, we can then say that

The $K_i$ is *normatively* the same as the $K_j$

if and only if

Every rule-matrix which holds of $K_i$ holds of $K_j$ and vice versa.

51.    Finally, to bring this long harangue to an end, we can distinguish pure rule bound sortals, pure descriptive sortals and mixed sortals as follows:

a pure rule bound sortal is one the meaning postulates for which are specified exclusively in terms of rule-matrices

x is a $K_{pr}$ ≡ 'Let [(x) x is a --- $\supset x$ be $M_i$'d]!' holds of $K_{pr}$s;

a pure descriptive sortal is one the meaning postulates for which are specified exclusively in terms of descriptive criteria

x is a $K_{pd}$ ≡ x is $\varphi_1, \dots \varphi_n$;

and, finally,

a mixed rule-bound and descriptive sortal is one the meaning postulates for which involve both descriptive contexts and rule-matrices.

With this apparatus, we can lay down the following principle (where 's' is a variable which takes dot-quoted substituends):

The $s_i$ is (normatively) the same as $s_j \equiv s_i$ and $s_j$ are pure rule-bound sortals and every rule matrix which holds of $s_i$ holds of $s_j$ and vice versa.

Thus,

The •rapid• is (normatively) the same as the •quick• $\equiv$ every rule-matrix which holds of •rapid•s holds of •quick•s and vice versa

at which point I refer you to the final three paragraphs of my letter of June 23 for a coda. Many of the points which I have just been making were foreshadowed in my original paper, "Abstract Entities,"[4] though they were not applied to the problems we have been discussing.

52.     I have tried to strike while the iron is hot, in the hope that at least a minor break-through can be made in the log jam, though we are still a long way from a complete resolution of the problems raised in your Pitt volume essay. I doubt if you can convince me at this late stage that my general project is misguided, but it would certainly be a dash of cold water if you were to find that what I have to say in this letter is completely off target.

Cordially,

Wilfrid Sellars

**NOTE**

53.     It might occur to the reader to wonder whether the context 'holds of ...', which occurs in the definitions in paragraph 51, is like the context 'true of ...', extensional. If it were, we would be back in the soup, for it would then be a logical truth that

$$(K_i)(K_j)\ K_i \equiv K_j \supset a \text{ holds of } K_i\text{s} \equiv a \text{ holds of } K_j\text{s}.$$

Once again, any two vacuous sorts would be the same. The reader should therefore

---

[4] Thus see the opening pages of section II of that paper.

note that, as introduced in (5), the context

  holds of Ks

is stipulated to be logically equivalent to a context in which 'K' is *mentioned* rather than *used*. Thus, '*a* holds of $K_i$s' should be placed as material mode for

  The formula obtained from the matrix *a* by replacing the appropriate variable with '$K_i$' holds.

54.    I pointed out that 'true of' is a special case of 'holds of' and, indeed, its distinctive feature is that the context '*a* is true of ...' is indeed extensional by virtue of its connection with the basic truth context "..." is true'. Thus even though (as we should) we construe '*a* is true of $K_i$', as material mode for

  The formula obtained from the matrix *a* by replacing the appropriate variable with '$K_i$' is true,

it can be shown that

  $(K_i \equiv K_j) \supset (a$ is true of $K_i \equiv a$ is true of $K_j)$.

For the left hand side, '$K_i \equiv K_j$', tells us that

  $(x)\ x \in K_i \equiv x \in K_j$

which entails, by virtue of the principle of extensionality, that

  $... K_i ... \equiv ... K_j ...$

where '...___...' is any context in which '$K_i$' and '$K_j$' occur properly; hence it also entails that the corresponding truth statements

  '... $K_i$ ...' is true; '... $K_j$ ...' is true

are equivalent, i.e., that

'... $K_i$ ...' is true $\equiv$ '... $K_j$ ...' is true

and hence, representing such a context by '*a*', that

*a* is true of $K_i$ $\equiv$ *a* is true of $K_j$.

**INDEX**

All references, except to the Preface, are by chapter and paragraph. For example, '1.7-9' refers to chapter 1, paragraphs 7 through 9. The Introduction is shown as 'I'; the Correspondence with Michael Loux, as 'C'.

# The Philosophical Works of Wilfrid Sellars

This bibliography is the most complete and correct bibliography of Sellars' work as of the date of publication. It contains corrections from Dr. Andrew Chrucky's web site on Sellars: (http://www.ditext.com/sellars/bib-s.html).

**Abbreviations**: *APQ* for *American Philosophical Quarterly*; *JP* for *The Journal of Philosophy*; *P&PR* for *Philosophy and Phenomenological Research*; *PREV* for *Philosophical Review*; *PSC* for *Philosophy of Science*; *PS* for *Philosophical Studies*; *ROM* for *Review of Metaphysics*.

PPE   1. "Pure Pragmatics and Epistemology," *PSC* 14 (1947): 181-202. In *PPPW* (112).

ENWW   2. "Epistemology and the New Way of Words," *JP* 44 (1947): 645-60. In *PPPW* (112).

RNWW   3. "Realism and the New Way of Words," *P&PR* 8 (1948): 601-34. Reprinted in *Readings in Philosophical Analysis*, edited by Herbert Feigl and Wilfrid Sellars (Appleton-Century-Crofts, 1949). In *PPPW* (112).

CIL   4. "Concepts as Involving Laws and Inconceivable without Them," *PSC* 15 (1948): 287-315. In *PPPW* (112).

APM   5. "Aristotelian Philosophies of Mind," in *Philosophy for the Future*, edited by Roy Wood Sellars, V.J. McGill, and Marvin Farber (The Macmillan Co., 1949): 544-70. In *KPT* (117).

LRB   6. "Language, Rules and Behavior," in *John Dewey: Philosopher of Science and Freedom*, edited by Sidney Hook (The Dial Press, 1949): 289-315. In *PPPW* (112).

LCP   7. "On the Logic of Complex Particulars," *Mind* 58 (1949): 306-38. In *PPPW* (112).

AD   8. "Acquaintance and Description Again," *JP* 46 (1949): 496-505.

RC   9. "Review of Ernest Cassirer, *Language and Myth*," *P&PR* 9 (1948-49): 326-29.

ILE   10. "The Identity of Linguistic Expressions and the Paradox of Analysis," *PS* 1 (1950): 24-31.

QMSP   11. "Quotation Marks, Sentences, and Propositions," *P&PR* 10 (1950): 515-25. In *PPPW* (112).

GQ   12. "Gestalt Qualities and the Paradox of Analysis," *PS* 1 (1950): 92-4.

OM   13. "Obligation and Motivation," *PS* 2 (1951): 21-25.

RP   14. "Review of Arthur Pap, *Elements of Analytic Philosophy*," *P&PR* 11 (1950): 104-9.

OMR   15. "Obligation and Motivation," in *Readings in Ethical Theory*, edited by Wilfrid Sellars and John Hospers (Appleton-Century-Crofts, 1952): 511-17. A revised and expanded version of *OM* (13).

RCA   16. "Review of C. West Churchman and Russell L. Ackoff, *Methods of Inquiry:*

An Introduction to Philosophy and Scientific Method," *P&PR* 11 (1951): 149-50.

CHT     17.  "Comments on Mr. Hempel's Theses," *ROM* 5 (1952): 623-25.

MMB     18.  "Mind, Meaning, and Behavior," *PS* 3 (1952): 83-95.

P       19.  "Particulars," *P&PR* 13 (1952): 184-99. In *SPR* (53).

ITSA    20.  "Is There a Synthetic A Priori?," *PSC* 20 (1953): 121-38. Reprinted in a revised form in *American Philosophers at Work*, edited by Sidney Hook (Criterion Press, 1957); also published in Italy in translation. In *SPR* (53).

SSMB    21.  "A Semantical Solution of the Mind-Body Problem," *Methodos* 5 (1953): 45-82. In *PPPW* (112).

IM      22.  "Inference and Meaning," *Mind* 62 (1953): 313-38. In *PPPW* (112).

PRE     23.  "Presupposing," *PREV* 63 (1954): 197-215. Reprinted in *Essays on Bertrand Russell*, edited by E.D. Klemke (Univ. of Illinois Press, 1970): 173-89.

SRLG    24.  "Some Reflections on Language Games," *PSC* 21 (1954): 204-28. A revised version is in *SPR* (53).

NPD     25.  "A Note on Popper's Argument for Dualism," *Analysis* 15 (1954): 23-4.

PR      26.  "Physical Realism," *P&PR* 15 (1955): 13-32. In *PPME* (102).

PSB     27.  "Putnam on Synonymity and Belief," *Analysis* 15 (1955): 117-20.

VTM     28.  "Vlastos and 'The Third Man'," *PREV* 64 (1955): 405-37. In *PPHP* (101).

IIO     29.  "Imperatives, Intentions, and the Logic of 'Ought'," *Methodos* 8 (1956): 228-68.

CE      30.  "The Concept of Emergence," (with Paul Meehl), in *Minnesota Studies in the Philosophy of Science*, Vol. I, edited by Herbert Feigl and Michael Scriven (University of Minnesota Press, 1956): 239-52.

EPM     31.  "Empiricism and the Philosophy of Mind," (Presented at the University of London in Special Lectures in Philosophy for 1956 under the title "The Myth of the Given: Three Lectures on Empiricism and the Philosophy of Mind"), *ibid.*, 253-329. In *SPR* (53).

LSPO    32.  "Logical Subjects and Physical Objects," *P&PR* 17 (1957): 458-72. Contribution to a symposium with Peter Strawson held at Duke University, November, 1955.

CDCM    33.  "Counterfactuals, Dispositions, and the Causal Modalities," in *Minnesota Studies in the Philosophy of Science*, Vol. II, edited by Herbert Feigl, Michael Scriven, and Grover Maxwell (University of Minnesota Press, 1958): 225-308.

ITM     34.  "Intentionality and the Mental," a symposium by correspondence with Roderick Chisholm, *ibid.*, 507-39. Reprinted in *Intentionality, Mind and Language*, edited by A. Marras (Univ. of Illinois Press, 1972).

SFA     35.  "Substance and Form in Aristotle," *JP* 54 (1957): 688-99. The opening paper in a symposium on Aristotle's conception of form held at the December, 1957 meeting of the American Philosophical Association. In *PPHP* (101).

EAE     36.  "Empiricism and Abstract Entities," in *The Philosophy of Rudolf Carnap (The Library of Living Philosophers)* edited by Paul A. Schilpp (Open Court,

1963): 431-68.

GE   37.   "Grammar and Existence: A Preface to Ontology," *Mind* 69 (1960): 499-533. Two lectures delivered at Yale University, March, 1958. In *SPR* (53). Reprinted in *The Problem of Universals*, edited by C. Landesman (Basic Books, 1971).

TWO   38.   "Time and the World Order," in *Minnesota Studies in the Philosophy of Science*, Vol. III, edited by Herbert Feigl and Grover Maxwell (University of Minnesota Press, 1962): 527-616. A Metaphysical and Epistmological Analysis of Becoming.

IIOR   39.   "Imperatives, Intentions, and the Logic of 'Ought'," in *Morality and the Language of Conduct*, a collection of essays in moral philosophy edited by Hector-Neri Castaneda and George Nakhnikian (Wayne State University Press, 1963): 159-214. A radically revised and enlarged version of *IIO* (29).

BBK   40.   "Being and Being Known," *Proceedings of the American Catholic Philosophical Association* (1960): 28-49. In *SPR* (53).

LT   41.   "The Language of Theories," in *Current Issues in the Philosophy of Science*, edited by Herbert Feigl and Grover Maxwell (Holt, Rinehart, and Winston, 1961): 57-77. In *SPR* (53). Reprinted in *The Problem of Scientific Realism*, edited by E.A. McKinnon (Appleton-Century-Crofts, 1972).

CM   42.   "Comments on Maxwell's "Meaning Postulates in Scientific Theories,"" *ibid.*, 183-92.

PSIM   43.   "Philosophy and the Scientific Image of Man," in *Frontiers of Science and Philosophy*, edited by Robert Colodny (University of Pittsburgh Press, 1962): 35-78. In *SPR* (53).

RMSS   44.   "Raw Materials, Subjects and Substrata," in *The Concept of Matter*, edited by Ernan McMullin (The University of Notre Dame Press, 1963): 259-72 and 276-80; remarks by Sellars on 55-7, 100-1, and 245-7. In *PPHP* (101).

CMM   45.   Comments on McMullin's "Matter as a Principle," *ibid.*, 209-13.

NS   46.   "Naming and Saying," *PSC* 29 (1962): 7-26. In *SPR* (53).

TC   47.   "Truth and Correspondence," *JP* 59 (1962): 29-56. In *SPR* (53).

AE   48.   "Abstract Entities," *ROM* 16 (1963): 627-71. In *PPME* (102).

CAE   49.   "Classes as Abstract Entities and the Russell Paradox," *ROM* 17 (1963): 67-90. Iin *PPME* (101).

PANF   50.   "The Paradox of Analysis: A Neo-Fregean Approach," *Analysis* Supplementary Vol. 24 (1964): 84-98. In *PPME* (102).

TE   51.   "Theoretical Explanation," in *Philosophy of Science: The Delaware Seminar*, Vol. II (John Wiley, 1963): 61-78. In *PPME* (102).

IRH   52.   "The Intentional Realism of Everett Hall," (in *Commonsense Realism: Critical Essays on the Philosophy of Everett W. Hall*, edited by E. M. Adams) *The Southern Journal of Philosophy* 4 (1966): 103-15. In *PPME* (102).

SPR   53.   *Science, Perception and Reality* (Routledge and Kegan Paul, 1963). Includes items (19), (20), (24), (31), (37), (40), (41), (43), (46), (47), and a hitherto unpublished essay, *PHM*, "Phenomenalism". Re-issued by Ridgeview

Publishing Company in 1991.

IV       54.    "Induction as Vindication," *PSC* 31 (1964): 197-231.

NI       55.    "Notes on Intentionality," *JP* 61 (1964): 655-65. Presented in a symposium on intentionality at the 1964 meeting of the American Philosophical Association (Eastern Division). In *PPME* (102). Reprinted in *Intentionality, Mind and Language*, edited by A. Marras (Univ. of Illinois Press, 1972).

IAMB    56.    "The Identity Approach to the Mind-Body Problem," *ROM* 18 (1965): 430-51. Presented at the Boston Colloquium for the Philosophy of Science, April, 1963. In *PPME* (102).

ML       57.    "Meditations Leibnitziennes," *APQ* 2 (1965): 105-18. An expanded version of the opening paper in a symposium on Rationalism at the May, 1958, meeting of the American Philosophical Association. In *PPHP* (101).

SRI      58.    "Scientific Realism or Irenic Instrumentalism: A Critique of Nagel and Feyerabend on Theoretical Explanation," *Boston Studies in the Philosophy of Science*, Vol. II, edited by Robert Cohen and Max Wartofsky (Humanities Press, 1965): 171-204. In *PPME* (102).

TA       59.    "Thought and Action," in *Freedom and Determinism*, edited by Keith Lehrer (Random House, 1966): 105-39.

FD       60.    "Fatalism and Determinism," *ibid.*, 141-74.

RPH      61.    "The Refutation of Phenomenalism: Prolegomena to a Defense of Scientific Realism," in P.K. Feyerabend and G. Maxwell (eds.), *Mind, Matter, and Method* (University of Minnesota Press, 1966).

PP       62.    *Philosophical Perspectives* (Charles C. Thomas, Publisher, 1967; reprinted in two volumes by Ridgeview Publishing Co.). Includes items (26), (28), (35), (44), (48), (49), (50), (51), (52), (55), (56), (57), (58), and *VTMR*, a rejoinder to Gregory Vlastos on the Third Man Argument, and three previously unpublished essays: *SC*, "The Soul as Craftsman" (on Plato's Idea of the Good), *AMI*, "Aristotle's Metaphysics: An Interpretation," and *SE*, "Science and Ethics."

SM       63.    *Science and Metaphysics: Variations on Kantian Themes*, The John Locke Lectures for 1965-66 (Routledge and Kegan Paul, 1967). Re-issued in 1992 by Ridgeview Publishing Company.

PH       64.    "Phenomenalism," in *Intentionality, Minds and Perception*, edited by H-N. Castaneda (Wayne State University Press, 1967): 215-74. A revised and abbreviated version of essay *PHM* (53).

RA       65.    "Reply to Aune," *ibid.*, 286-300.

FCET    66.    *Form and Content in Ethical Theory*, The Lindley Lecture for 1967 (Department of Philosophy, University of Kansas, 1967). In *SM* (63).

KTE      67.    "Some Remarks on Kant's Theory of Experience," *JP* 64 (1967): 633-47. Presented in a symposium on Kant at the 1967 meeting of the American Philosophical Association (Eastern Division).In *KTM* (118).

MP       68.    "Metaphysics and the Concept of a Person," in *The Logical Way of Doing Things*, edited by Karel Lambert (Yale University Press, 1969): 219-52. In *KTM* (118).

SRTT   69. "Some Reflections on Thoughts and Things," *Nous* 1 (1967): 97-121. Reprinted as Chapter III of *SM* (63).

CDI    70. "Reflection on Contrary to Duty Imperatives," *Nous* 1 (1967): 303-44.

KSU    71. "Kant's Views on Sensibility and Understanding," *Monist* 51 (1967): 463-91. Reprinted as Chapter I of *SM* (63). The first of the six John Locke Lectures.

SPB    72. "Some Problems about Belief," in *Philosophical Logic*, edited by J. W. Davis, D. T. Hockney, and W. K. Wilson (D. Reidel, 1969): 46-65. Reprinted in *Words and Objections: Essays on the Work of W.V. Quine*, edited by D. Davidson and J. Hintikka (D. Reidel, 1969): 186-205.

NDL    73. "Are There Non-deductive Logics?" in *Essays in Honor of Carl G. Hempel*, edited by Nicholas Rescher *et al.*, *Synthese Library* (D. Reidel, 1970): 83-103.

LTC    74. "Language as Thought and as Communication," *P&PR* 29 (1969): 506-27. Reprinted in *Language and Human Nature*, edited by P. Kurtz (Warren H. Green, 1971) with commentary by M. Dufrenne, E. Morot-Sir, J. Margolis, and E.S. Casey.

KBDW   75. "On Knowing the Better and Doing the Worse," *International Philosophical Quarterly*, 10 (1970): 5-19. The 1969 Suarez Philosophy Lecture delivered at Fordham University. In *KTM* (118).

SSIS   76. "Science, Sense Impressions, and Sensa: A Reply to Cornman," *ROM* 25 (1971): 391-447.

TTC    77. "Towards a Theory of the Categories," *Experience and Theory*, edited by L. Foster and J.W. Swanson (University of Massachusetts Press, 1970): 55-78. In *KTM* (118).

AAE    78. "Actions and Events," *Nous* 7 (1973): 179-202. Contribution to a symposium on the topic at the University of North Carolina, November, 1969.

SK     79. "The Structure of Knowledge: (1) Perception; (2) Minds; (3) Epistemic Principles," The Matchette Foundation Lectures for 1971 at the University of Texas. Published in *Action, Knowledge and Reality: Studies in Honor of Wilfrid Sellars*, edited by Hector-Neri Castañeda (Bobbs-Merrill, 1975): 295-347.

RAL    80. "Reason and the Art of Living in Plato," in *Phenomenology and Natural Existence: Essays in Honor of Marvin Farber*, edited by Dale Riepe (The University of New York Press, 1973): 353-77.

I      81. "...this I or he or it (the thing) which thinks," the presidential address, American Philosophical Association (Eastern Division), for 1970, *Proceedings of the American Philosophical Association* 44 (1972): 5-31. In *KTM* (118).

RD     82. "Reply to Donagan," an essay on fatalism and determinism (1971). *PS* 27 (1975): 149-84.

OPM    83. "Ontology and the Philosophy of Mind in Russell," in *Bertrand Russell's Philosophy*, edited by George Nakhnikian (Duckworth, and Barnes and Noble, 1974): 57-100.

RM     84. "Reply to Marras," *Canadian Journal of Philosophy* 2 (1973): 485-93.

CC     85. "Conceptual Change," in *Conceptual Change*, edited by P. Maynard and G.

Pearce (D. Reidel, 1973): 77-93.

RQ      86.  "Reply to Quine," *Synthese* 26 (1973): 122-45.

AR      87.  "Autobiographical Reflections: (February, 1973)." Published in *Action, Knowledge and Reality*, edited by H.-N. Castañeda (Bobbs-Merrill, 1975): 277-93.

DKMB    88.  "The Double-Knowledge Approach to the Mind-Body Problem," *The New Scholasticism* 45 (1971): 269-89.

MFC     89.  "Meaning as Functional Classification (A Perspective on the Relation of Syntax to Semantics)," (with replies to Daniel Dennett and Hilary Putnam) *Synthese* 27 (1974): 417-37. Reprinted in *Intentionality, Language and Translation*, edited by J.G. Troyer and S.C. Wheeler, III (D. Reidel, 1974). An expanded version of *BEB*, "Belief and the Expression of Belief", in *Language, Belief, and Metaphysics*, edited by H.E. Kiefer and M.K. Munitz (State University of New York Press, 1970): 146-158.

RDP     90.  "Reply to Dennett and Putnam" *Synthese* 27 (1974): 457-446. Reprinted in *Intentionality, Language and Translation*, edited by J.G. Troyer and S.C. Wheeler, III (D. Reidel, 1974).

IAE     91.  "On the Introduction of Abstract Entities," in *Forms of Representation*, Proceedings of the 1972 Philosophy Colloquium of the University of Western Ontario, edited by B. Freed, A. Marras and P. Maynard (North Holland, 1975): 47-74.

GEC     92.  "Givenness and Explanatory Coherence," (presented at a symposium on Foundations of Knowledge at the 1973 meeting of the American Philosophical Association (Eastern Division)). An abbreviated version is in *JP* 70 (1973): 612-24.

SSS     93.  "Seeing, Seeming, and Sensing," in *The Ontological Turn: Studies in the Philosophy of Gustav Bergmann*, ed. by M.S. Gram and E.D. Klemke (University of Iowa Press, 1974): 195-210. The first in a series of three Matchette Lectures (79).

EPH     94.  *Essays in Philosophy and its History* (D. Reidel, 1974). Includes items (36), (49), (51), (54), (67), (68), (72), (73), (74), (75), (77), (78), (80), (81), (84), (85), (86), and (91).

BD      95.  "Berkeley and Descartes: Reflections on the 'New Way of Ideas'" (presented in 1974 in the Program in the History and Philosophy of Theories of Perception at Ohio State University). Published in *Studies in Perception: Interpretations in the History of Philosophy and Science*, edited by Peter K. Machamer and Robert G. Turnbull (Ohio State University Press, 1977): 259-311. In *KTM* (118).

ATS     96.  "The Adverbial Theory of the Objects of Sensation," in *Metaphilosophy* 6, edited by Terrell Bynum (Basil Blackwell, 1975): 144-60.

VR      97.  "Volitions Re-affirmed," *Action Theory*, edited by Myles Brand and Douglas Walton (D. Reidel, 1976): 47-66. Presented at a conference on action theory at Winnipeg, May, 1975.

*KTI* 98. "Kant's Transcendental Idealism" (presented at an International Kant Congress at the University of Ottawa). Published in volume 6, *Collections of Philosophy* (1976): 165-181. In *KTM* (118).

*SRT* 99. "Is Scientific Realism Tenable?" (presented at a symposium at the 1976 Philosophy of Science Association Meeting in Chicago). Published in volume II, *Proceedings of PSA* (1976): 307-334.

*MMM* 100. "Hochberg on Mapping, Meaning, and Metaphysics," in *Midwest Studies in Philosophy II*, edited by Peter French, Theodore Vehling, Jr., and Howard Wettstein (University of Minnesota Press, 1977): 214-24.

*PPHP* 101. *Philosophical Perspectives: History of Philosophy* (Ridgeview Publishing Co., 1977). A reprint of Part I of *Philosophical Perspectives* (62). Includes items (28), (35), (44), (57) and *VTMR*, a rejoinder to Gregory Vlastos on the Third Man Argument, *SC*, "The Soul as Craftsman" (on Plato's Idea of the Good), and *AMI*, "Aristotle's Metaphysics: An Interpretation."

*PPME* 102. *Philosophical Perspectives: Metaphysics and Epistemology* (Ridgeview Publishing Co., 1977). A reprint of Part II of *Philosophical Perspectives* (62). Includes items (26), (48), (49), (50), (51), (52), (55), (56), (58), and *SE*, "Science and Ethics."

*IKTE* 103. "The Role of Imagination in Kant's Theory of Experience," The Dotterer Lecture 1978 in *Categories: A Colloquium*, edited by Henry W. Johnstone, Jr. (Pennsylvania State University): 231-45. In *KTM* (118).

*NAO* 104. *Naturalism and Ontology* (Ridgeview Publishing Co., 1980). The John Dewey Lectures for 1973-4. Reprinted with corrections in 1997.

*MGEC* 105. "More on Givenness and Explanatory Coherence," in *Justification and Knowledge*, edited by George Pappas (D. Reidel, 1979): 169-182.

*SRPC* 106. "Some Reflections on Perceptual Consciousness," in *Selected Studies in Phenomenology and Existential Philosophy*, edited by R. Bruzina and B. Wilshire (1977): 169-185. In *KTM* (118).

*ORAV* 107. "On Reasoning About Values," *APQ* 17 (1980): 81-101. One of three Tsanoff Lectures presented at Rice University, October 1978.

*SSOP* 108. "Sensa or Sensings: Reflections on the Ontology of Perception," *PS* 41 (Essays in Honor of James Cornman) (1982): 83-111. Presented at a Colloquium at the University of North Carolina, October 1976.

*BLM* 109. "Behaviorism, Language and Meaning," *Pacific Philosophical Quarterly* 61 (1980): 3-30.

*FMPP* 110. "Foundations for a Metaphysics of Pure Process" (The Carus Lectures) *The Monist* 64 (1981): 3-90

*CPCI* 111. "Conditional Promises and Conditional Intentions (Including a Reply to Castañeda)," in *Agent, Language and the Structure of the World: Essays Presented to Hector-Neri Castaneda, With His Replies*, edited by James E. Tomberlin (Hackett Publishing Co., 1983): 195-221.

*PPPW* 112. *Pure Pragmatics and Possible Worlds: The Early Essays of Wilfrid Sellars*, edited and introduced by Jeffrey F. Sicha (Ridgeview Publishing Co., 1980).

Includes items (1), (2), (3), (4), (6), (7), (11), (21), and (22).

MEV    113.    "Mental Events," *Philosophical Studies* 39 (1981): 325-45. Contributed to a symposium of that title at the 1980 meeting of American Philosophical Association (Western Division).

TTP    114.    "Towards a Theory of Predication," in *How Things Are*, edited by James Bogen and James McGuire (Reidel, 1983): 281-318. Presented at a conference on predication at Pitzer College in April, 1981.

OAFP    115.    "On Accepting First Principles," in *Philosophical Perspectives, 2, Epistemology, 1988*, edited by James E. Tomberlin (Ridgeview Publishing Co., (1988): 301-14. This paper was written in the sixties but first published here. In *KTM* (118).

ME    116.    *The Metaphysics of Epistemology: Lectures by Wilfrid Sellars*, edited by P.V. Amaral (Ridgeview Publishing Co., 1989).

KPT    117.    *Kant and Pre-Kantian Themes: Lectures by Wilfrid Sellars*, edited by P.V. Amaral (Ridgeview Publishing Co., 2002). In addition to Sellars' Kant lectures, this volume includes lectures on Descartes, Locke, Spinoza (with an introduction by the editor), Leibniz, and a reprint of *APM* (5).

KTM    118.    *Kant's Transcendental Metaphysics: Sellars' Cassirer Lectures and Other Essays*, edited and introduced by Jeffrey F. Sicha (Ridgeview Publishing Co., 2002). In addition to Sellars' notes for his Cassirer Lectures (*CLN*), this volume includes items (67), (68), (75), (77), (81), (95), (98), (103), (106), (115) and *OAPK*, Part I of the unpublished essay whose Part II is (67). (This unpublished essay is listed as entry "1970" in *Circulated Papers and Lectures*. It was actually written in 1966 or 1967, but revised in 1970, or perhaps, late 1969.)

OAPK    119.    *OAPK* is Part I of the unpublished essay whose Part II is (67). Published in *KTM*.

CLN    120.    Sellars' notes for his Cassirer Lectures, published in *KTM*.

WSNDL121.    *Wilfrid Sellars Notre Dame Lectures 1969-1986*, edited by P.V. Amaral (Ridgeview Publishing Company, 2015.)

SMCN    122.    *Notes from Wilfrid Sellars Metaphysics Lectures 1973-1974*, edited by P.V. Amaral (Kindle, 2015).

*Additional Works by Wilfrid Sellars* (compiled by P. V. Amaral)

*Philosophical Letters*

1961    To Bruce Aune, October 19, 1961.
Analysis and explanation of minimal actions and theoretical reduction.
*To Sellars from Aune, October 23, 1961.*
1961    To Bruce Aune, November 11, 1961.
1964    To Jack Smart, March 9, 1964.
A discussion of Theoretical Reduction.

*To Sellars from Smart, February 27, 1964.*
*To Sellars from Smart, March 14, 1964.*
1965   To David Rosenthal, September 3, 1965.
     The origin of the mental in *NI, SRLG* and *IM*.
     *To Sellars from Rosenthal, July 6, 1965.*
1965   To David Rosenthal, September 8, 1965.
     *To Sellars from Rosenthal, October 2, 1965.*
     *To Sellars from Rosenthal, December 17, 1965.*
1966   To David Rosenthal, January 4, 1966.
1967   To Ruth Barcan Marcus, August 21, 1967.
     The relation of modality and metalanguage.
1970   To Gilbert Harman, February 26, 1970.
     On Harman's review of *SM*.
     *To Sellars from Harman, March 24, 1970.*
1970   To Gilbert Harman, November 20, 1970.
1971   To Annette Baier, November 30, 1971.
     A discussion of *SPB*.
     *To Sellars from Baier, November 29, 1971.*
1972   To Jay Rosenberg, July 25, 1972.
     *To Sellars from Rosenberg, August 29, 1972.*
1972   To Jay Rosenberg, September 5, 1972.
     A clarification of *AE* and the classification of events as objects.
     *From Rosenberg to Sellars, September 28, 1972.*
1972   To Annette Baier, January 12, 1972.
     *To Sellars from Baier, February 7, 1972.*
1973   To Jay Rosenberg, January 16, 1973.
1974   To Roderick Firth, April 16, 1974.
1974   To Roderick Firth, February 12, 1974.
1974   To Roderick Firth, January 22, 1974.
     The exchange explores the anti-Cartesian account of sensing and its role in perceiving
     (*EPM, SK*).
     *To Sellars from Firth, February 22, 1974.*
     *To Sellars from Firth, February 2, 1974.*
     *To Sellars from Firth, January 13, 1974.*
1975   To Bruce Aune, June 23, 1975.
     On the logic of Ought-to-do's and *CDI*.
1975   To Ausonio Marras, November 26, 1975.
     On the theoretical character of common sense: *EPM, EAE* and *ITM*.
1978   To Michael Loux, June 23, 2978 (reprinted in *NAO*).
1978   To Michael Loux, November 6, 1978 (reprinted in *NAO*).
     *To Sellars from Loux, October 6, 1978.*
1979   To Bruce Aune, April 30, 1979.
     On the concept of dependent implication.

*To Sellars from Aune, May 15, 1979*
*To Sellars from Aune, June 9, 1979.*
1979    To Judith Thomson, June 6, 1979
A discussion of *IIO* and *ORAV.*
*To Sellars from Thompson, May 25, 1979.*

*Circulated Papers and Lectures*

1959    "Inferencia y significado," *Separata de la Revista Universidad de San Carlos,* number 50, Guatemala, C. A. ("Inference and Meaning" translated by by Hector-Neri Castañeda).
1964    "Introduction to the Philosophy of Science," Lectures given at the Summer Institute for the History of Philosophy of Science at The American University, Washington, D.C., June, 1964.
1966    "'Ought' and Moral Principles," February 14, 1966.
1967    "Fatalism and Determinism," a revised version of *FD* (60), 1966.
1967    "Belief and the Expression of Belief," circulated on December 31, 1967, and later incorporated into *LTC* (73), 1969.
1968    "Reason and the Art of Living in Plato," printed as *RAL* (79), a paper presented in a conference held at Ohio State University, April 5, 1968.
1970    "Ontology, the A Priori and Kant," Part one: introduction, 1970.
1971    "Practical Reasoning Again: Notes for a revision of Thought and Action," August, 1971.
1976    "Is Scientific Realism Tenable?," July 30, 1976, a prelimary draft of *SRT* (97), 1976.
1976    "Kant and Pre-Kantian Philosophy," university lectures on *The Critique of Pure Reason* and its historical framework: Descartes, Leibniz, Spinoza and Hume. May-June, 1976. (Now published as *KPT* (117).)
1977    "Symposium on Materialism," transcripts of a discussion on materialism: Wilfrid Sellars, George Pappas, William Lycan and Robert Turnbull.

Made in the USA
Las Vegas, NV
15 March 2024

87268465R00115